TOP 10 QUALITIES OF A GREAT LEADER

By

Phil Pringle

Harrison House
Tulsa, Oklahoma

12 11 10 09 08   10 9 8 7 6 5 4 3 2

Top 10 Qualities of a Great Leader
ISBN 13: 978-1-57794-939-8
ISBN 10: 1-57794-939-0
Copyright © 2007 by Phil Pringle
Locked Bag 8
Dee Why, NSW 2099
Australia www.ccc.org.au

Published by Harrison House Publishers
P.O. Box 35035
Tulsa, Oklahoma 74153 www.harrisonhouse.com

Contents

Introduction

In Titus 1:5, Paul reminds Titus that he left him in Crete to "...*set in order things that are lacking....*" He also reminds him to "...*appoint elders* [minister-leaders] *in every city....*" There's a revolution in this verse. This is leadership operating at its premium. Paul is arranging to impact and transform an entire nation by affecting every city, town, and village.

It's important for us to understand that Cretans had a general reputation for being liars and evil beasts and for laziness, gluttony, and other vices (see Titus 1:12). In secular history, they were known for their cunning deception, ambush tactics, and archery. Even in some societies today, to call someone a "Cretan" is to deride him as unlikable.

God positions us in dark situations so we can bring transformation. Titus, in Crete, is like you or I in a strife-torn family, an unjust employment situation, a dark neighbourhood, a difficult apartment block, a turbulent company, a town we don't like, a suburb that challenges us, or a culture we're uncomfortable in. Paul left Titus there to change things, to bring in the kingdom.

Note that the apostle instructs Titus to appoint leaders in every *city,*not every church. Not every city of Crete had a church! The strategy was to send a leader into each city, anticipating they would assume an authority over that city, create a church, and transform the place. God has left us in whatever place we are in with the same purpose—to transform it.

Obviously, such leaders needed to be of a certain breed. In Titus 1:6-9 Paul lists the character qualities that determined the criteria by which Titus was to select these leaders of cities. These people would have been disciples under Titus before being released into this calling. Therefore, it became his task to train and appraise the potential leaders according to Paul's requirements.

Titus had to identify what was lacking even though the Cretans had been touched by God on the day of Pentecost (see Acts 2), and the apostle Paul himself had had a brief initial influence on the isle of Crete (see Acts 27). With his book *Natural Church Development,* Christian A. Schwarz has helped the church immensely by identifying eight essential qualities that provide an environment for the activation of God's natural growth "automatons" (processes). It is well worth reading, research-ing, and acting upon the material in *Natural Church Development.* After surveying 1,000 churches initially and having now consulted 40,000 churches worldwide—both growing and non-growing—the following eight elements emerged as essential[1]:

1. Empowering leadership

2. Passionate spirituality

3. Gift-based serving

4. Inspiring worship services

5. Functional structure

6. Holistic small groups

7. Need-oriented evangelism

8. Love

Each of these can be expanded to a wider and fuller description. According to Schwarz's research, each of the eight qualities must exceed a quota of 65 percent to be effective in causing real growth in a church. With a measure such as this, it is not that difficult to identify "things that are lacking." This research obviously relates to existing churches. However, Titus had the burden of setting in place leaders in cities where there were no churches, and therefore needed to create something from nothing. This is a calling that apostolic authority is gifted to implement—the birthing of churches.

The very first quality Paul says the leader must have is not preaching ability, vision, faith, management skills, people skills, team-building skills, or decision-making skills (all of which are essential leadership traits). Rather, Paul says the first quality of the leader is that he must have a good reputation in the marketplace, in the community. He must have good references from local businesses and other community leaders. He is a person who lives with integrity, who pays his bills, and who commands respect by a life well lived. If he didn't have this quality of character, then he would be a blockage to people trusting and coming to the church. The kind of people who would gather around him would also be blockages. But if he is of good character and has earned the trust of the city, then his disciples will be the same—he will gather the same kind of people. In short, the leader must be a bridge between the city and the church.

Titus was left in Crete with a trust and a command. Because he was obedient to Paul's instructions, those under him would also carry the same spirit of respecting a chain of command. This is a powerful key for us to grasp in the basics of leadership formation, so let's go deeper on this point.

Leaders—What Lies Beneath?

You the Leader...hmmm! I wrote that book ten years ago. I am tempted to call this book "You the Follower." It didn't used to be the case, but we now have a lot of information on leadership. The notion of leadership attracts the naive. I have a nagging suspicion—no, I'm convinced—that our picture of leadership is incomplete. I've attempted to teach leadership every week to our staff, leaders, and workers all around the world, in my cell groups, in our ministry training colleges, at conferences, and in church meetings. My growing conviction is that leadership is actually built not on leading but on "followership."

The quality of our leadership is directly proportionate to the quality of our followership. Note, I didn't say our *ability,* but rather our *quality.* Some leaders have no idea how to follow. Perhaps they simply inherited a position of leadership. People follow them because they have to, not because they want to. This kind of leadership, however long it lasts, will always be flawed. My effectiveness as a leader lies in the fact that I myself also have a leader and can be led. Obedience equals effectiveness! Our capacity as leaders is determined by our capacity to serve. The leader serves not just God but people. Our strength of influence is directly proportionate to our level of submission not just to God, but also to those people whom God places in our world. The centurion asking Jesus to heal his servant (see Matt. 8:9) knows that his authority over his soldiers rests on his subjection to Rome. He sees Jesus in the same light. As Jesus is subject to God (the Healer), He therefore has power to command healing.

In the movie *The Rock,* a military general played by Ed Harris decides to correct injustices by attacking San Francisco using soldiers under his command. As the story progresses, his authority is increasingly questioned until his soldiers finally turn on him. He loses his authority because he is not submitted to any higher authority—he is no longer a follower. None of us has any authority of our own. All authority comes from God (see Rom. 13:1). He provides lines of command through which that authority flows from Him to us. When we are submitted to authority, we become empowered.

Our call to lead is not a call to assume authority over people. The Bible opposes this, as stated in 1 Peter 5:3: "...*nor as being lords over those entrusted to you....*" (1 Peter 5:3). Rather, all believers are called to place themselves under authority, "...*submit yourselves to your elders...*" (1 Peter 5:5). A leader has only as much authority as the people he or she leads are willing to give him or her.

Followership is more rare than it should be. Many feel they are beyond being led by anyone except God. This attitude effectively renders all other counsel irrelevant. Yet God elects to impact our lives through His servants, our leaders. If we tread a path based solely on personal revelation, ignoring the guidance of others, we've joined a very flaky crowd headed for a dangerous destination.

The inclination to follow is in the nature of the believer. We are transformed from the cantankerous goat nature to the agreeable sheep nature when we are born again. This is reflected in our ability to be influenced by others.

No one is the leader in every situation or season of life. Sometimes we are a follower, sometimes a manager, and other times a leader. We need the capacity to accept whatever role a given situation demands. No leaders will be successful without having proven they can accept authority over their own lives in their formative stages. We will always have people to submit to and others whom we lead.

We are His sheep. (Ps. 100:3.) Sheep are meek and therefore vulnerable. This vulnerability needs a defense, but it is wisdom not violence. His sheep are harmless as doves, yet wise as serpents. (Matt. 10:16.) A deep characteristic of this wisdom is teachability. Wisdom learns all the time (see Prov. 1:5). This is followership. This is where our guidance and safety lie.

The "follower-leader" is easily discoverable in three callings: servant, soldier, and son. These three traits are obvious in great leaders and painfully absent in unsuccessful leaders.

1

SERVING WILL SERVE YOU WELL

Building the church is God's great project on earth. In our church, every message and event is designed to build our church. The messages become the culture of our church. What we preach today is a seed that becomes a full-grown tree tomorrow. "Followership" and servanthood are high-priority messages (seeds we plant) because they build the culture of the kingdom of God. This builds the church because the house of God is built on serving. When people join our church, we tell them they are now members of a house, not a hotel. Rather than expecting to be served as in a hotel, we expect them to accept a serving role to help grow, build, and maintain the house.

> *"You looked for much, but indeed it came to little; and when you brought it home, I blew it away. Why?" says the Lord of hosts. "Because of My house that is in ruins, while every one of you runs to his own house."*
>
> Haggai 1:9

If we neglect His house in favor of our own house, then our efforts will vaporize. When His house is our first priority, however, we bring favor to our own.

The greatest curse in the world today is self-centeredness. A New York phone company surveyed 500 telephone conversations. What was the most common word? "I"—it occurred 3,900 times in the five hundred calls.

...in the last days perilous times will come: For men will be lovers of themselves....

2 Timothy 3:1-2

Looking up "troubled times" on the Internet, it seems that everything but self-centeredness is blamed for perilous times—guns, drugs, economic downturns, changes of governments, fanatics in the Middle East, terrorists, weather patterns, global warming, El Niño, business monopolies, illiteracy, poverty, family breakdowns, violence, lawless media, hard-line religious groups, insensitive governments, road rage, high medical fees, interest rates, floods, tsunamis, bank charges, dot. com failures, and of course, wild animals are blamed for all kinds of problems we face today. However, the above scripture reveals that the real cause of perilous times is flawed character, not dire circumstances.

The character flaws Paul lists in 2 Timothy 3:2-9 spring from self-centered living. The shocking reality concerning this dark list of flaws is that Paul states these people have a "form of godliness"—they go to church!

To claim to be Christian means we claim to live unselfish lives. Great character springs from unselfishness. We bless others at our own expense. For many people, their world is all about them. Everything is always about them and what they're doing. But God created our universe to orbit around His Son, Jesus Christ, not ourselves:

...All things were created **through Him and for Him.**

Colossians 1:16

In 1611, the astronomer Galileo visited Rome to demonstrate the telescope to the papal court. He presented a theory contesting the popular belief of the day that everything revolves around the earth. He said he could prove this was not true. He submitted the teaching of another scientist, Copernicus, who believed that everything actually revolves around the sun. In 1616, the system of Copernicus was denounced as being dangerous to faith. Galileo was summoned to Rome and warned not to uphold or teach it. However, in 1632 he published a work supporting the Copernican system (as opposed to the Ptolemaic system). This marked a major turning point in scientific and philosophical thought.

Summoned once again to Rome, Galileo was tried in 1633 by the Inquisition and was brought to the point of making an abjuration of all beliefs and writings that held that the sun was the central body and the earth a moving body revolving around it with the other planets. Since 1761, accounts of the trial have reported that Galileo, as he arose from his knees, exclaimed sotto voce, *"E pur si muove"* ["nevertheless, it does move"]. After the Inquisition trial, Galileo was sentenced to an enforced residence in Siena.

It's astonishing that we continue to imagine that everything revolves around us, that we squirm from any other view even though it's plainly visible. Some of the scientists of Galileo's day refused to look through the telescope, holding what they believed to be true no matter what contradictory evidence might be presented. The opposers strengthened their denial through ignorance, not prepared to accept anything that challenged their precious beliefs.

Nevertheless, eventually truth irresistibly surfaces. Copernicus's proposition is a commonly accepted reality today.

Just as the earth orbits the sun, we are called to orbit Christ. He is our center. This is the fixed order of creation. When we accept this, we establish Christ as our ruler.

According to the revelator John, all things have been created for God's pleasure (see Rev. 4:11).

When parents are anticipating the arrival of a baby, they furnish a room, buy clothing, bedding, and everything else needed. They prepare for their new child. God did a similar thing in preparing for His Son, except He didn't just prepare a room. He created an entire universe filled with solar systems, stars, and planets, including planet earth with its trees, animals, and oceans. All the palms, oaks, and cedars; all the birds, cattle, horses, sheep, whales, and crayfish; all the waves, mountains, snow, and sunshine; all the nations, cultures, and people of all tribes and colors—all has been created for Him. This includes you and me. We have been created for God!

If we want to please God, we will try to be in harmony with this order. We fit into His plan, not He into ours. His pleasure is to bless us. He can do this when we put Him first in our personal world. In an ego-driven world, God-first living deals a fatal blow to self-centered living. There is no better life available than one lived for the ultimate Ruler of all.

Let's not shout *amen* just yet though. Such a lifestyle calls for changes. This is not just theory. We actually have to change how we live life so that we are not first in our world, but rather Christ is. Here are a few practical ways to do this:

1. Try getting through today without talking about yourself and what you're doing. Instead, ask others about themselves and what they're doing.

2. Try listening to someone else's story without talking about the same thing that happened to you (even though yours might be bigger, better, longer, nastier…).

3. Once every day for the next week, help someone else get what he or she wants. And let it mean you're not going to be able to do what you want.

4. Go to church with a view of seeing what you can give rather than what you can get.

5. Write your results in your journal.

Changing from a self-centered life to a Christ-centered life is not difficult if we simply die to ourselves and accept the life of someone who lives for another.

> *…whoever desires to become great among you shall be your servant. And whoever of you desires to be first shall be slave of all. For even the Son of Man did not come to be served, but to serve, and to give His life as a ransom for many.*
>
> Mark 10:43-45

In this lifestyle, we help others at our expense, when it is inconvenient to us. When we move from a life of comfort to life with discomfort, serving others even though it costs us time and money, we have embraced the kingdom of God.

Serve God and not serve people? Impossible! Serving people is serving God. If we're unable to serve people, we can't serve God.

Successful businesses understand the power of servanthood. As Jim Rohn says, "One customer, well taken care of, can be more valuable than $10,000 worth of advertising."[1]In her book on Australian business, *Good Service Is Good Business,* best-selling author Catherine DeVrye, a former IBM executive and Australian Executive Woman of the Year says,

In the future, it is estimated that 70 percent of the workforce will be involved in the service sector. If this prediction is even close to being correct, Australians had better quickly dispense with the idea that "service" equates to "subservience"—that serving people is an undignified way of making a living and is below our dignity.[2]

Insecurity stops us from serving others. We all prefer to be the important person, rather than the lesser. John 13 unfolds the startling record of when Jesus washed His disciples' feet. Washing feet ranked among the most undignified tasks of a servant. Yet we see Jesus doing this with dignity. He was secure in Himself. He cared not what others might think. He knew things. John 13:1 tells us that Jesus knew His hour, He knew what He had been given, He knew from where He had come, and He knew where He was going. He had no problem serving His own disciples. When we're secure, we can take on any role, even though it might threaten our importance. Security is the climate of a healthy soul. We know what we have, what our time is, where we are coming from, and where we are going. This confidence provides an internal climate of security. Thus we serve.

The Four Directions of Servanthood

1. Serving God

Serving God is doing His will, not ours.

There is a story about President Abraham Lincoln having once bought a slave girl with the sole purpose of giving her her freedom. She didn't realize why he was buying her. She thought she was simply being bought as a slave. He paid the price, then handed her her papers of freedom, but she didn't understand. "You are free," he told her. "Free?" she asked. "Can I go wherever I want to go now?" "Indeed you can," he said. "Then," she said, "if I am free to go anywhere, I will stay with you, and serve you until I die."

Israel's Old Testament calendar required that a Year of Jubilee be celebrated every 50 years. As part of the celebration, every slave was emancipated. However, if a slave did not want his freedom, preferring to remain with his owner, then his ear would be pierced; and he would wear an earring for the rest of his life, signifying that he had chosen slavery over freedom. (Ex. 21:5,6.)

When we receive Christ, God sets us free. The most natural response is to use that freedom to serve Him. We want to live with Him. We surrender to Him to be His "slave" forever. He "nails our ear to the door" as it were. We are spoiled for anything else in life. We have given our life and all our days to be His slave. This is basic to becoming a servant of God.

2. Serving leaders

The second direction of servanthood is serving men and women of God. The apostle Paul calls Timothy a son who has served him in the gospel:

> ...as a son with his father he served with me in the gospel.
>
> Philippians 2:22

Timothy served Paul, Joshua served Moses, Elisha served Elijah, and David served Saul. There is always someone with whom we are called to serve, a person and his or her vision. We are called to help them achieve their purpose. For the most part these are wonderful people. However, there are also leaders who are difficult to serve. It's an understatement to say that David found his leader, Saul, difficult. Saul tried to murder his young servant David many times. Yet this was the secret to the forging of great strength in the future king. These are crucial seed times in our lives. The way we treat those who are over us becomes the way we are treated by those we lead in later years. We reap what we sow! If we help people achieve their vision, others will help us to achieve ours.

I once heard a story about a young employee who was not trained in anything and had no educational qualifications, but who loved his work at the service station pumping gas, cleaning windows, and tidying the yard. He would arrive early to prepare the washroom and get everything ready for the day, and he would leave late, making sure everything was locked up.

The service station owner, who had no family, unexpectedly passed away. In his will, he left the station not to the head mechanic, not to the bookkeeper, not to the apprentices, but to the inexperienced, unqualified lad who had always gone the extra mile in serving the boss and the thing he loved—his garage.

There will always be people we are called to serve, whom we will help to accomplish their purposes. Mentoring is vital to success. However, this involves more than just chatting with a more experienced person. The mentoring relationship is opened up through serving. People sometimes ask me to mentor them. All they need do is to help me do what I do, and they'll find themselves in my world.

They'll learn more by serving than by any other means. A good "mentee" makes a great mentor. No matter how good a person's coach might be, if the person has no heart to serve and to learn, then they will fail to be coached.

3. Serving each other

...through love serve one another.

Galatians 5:13

After Jesus washed the feet of His disciples, He commanded them to do the same to each other. This is not really about washing feet. It's about serving one another.

In the business world, it's not the company that provides job security—only customers can do that! If customers are well served they come back; if not, they don't. Serving people means solving their problems.

Catherine DeVrye also relates that:

Research from Wharton Business School shows that 95 percent of customers who have a complaint handled efficiently and promptly will not only continue to do business with an organization but will become even more brand loyal. It costs five times more to obtain a new customer than to retain an existing one. It is critical that every-one in our organization understands the role each of us plays in keeping existing customers. It is critical to genuinely care about each and every customer. Customers appreciate quality and service long after they have forgotten the price or cost to them. Organizations that are prospering not only talk quality, they deliver it continually.[3]

Service focused companies go out of their way to hear customer complaints. Most customers—96 percent, in fact—don't bother to complain to the goods or service provider; they simply take their business elsewhere. No news is not necessarily good news. If we want to be effective in providing answers to people's problems, we need to identify what those problems are. How do we find out? We ask!

Serving each other opens us up to a world of relationships that bring success into our lives.

4. Serving all

I have made myself a servant to all, that I might win the more.

1 Corinthians 9:19

Instead of selling Jesus, we should try serving Him to people. Instead of just witnessing to people, we need to *be* a witness. Francis of Assisi is attributed as saying, "Preach the Gospel always, and if necessary, use words."

Serving is helping people at personal cost to ourselves. It involves sacrifice. We send medical teams from our church to refugee camps in Indonesia to treat people with tuberculosis and to prevent others from contracting the disease. When we invite these people to receive Christ, they do so happily. Those who have understood the power of serving other people can tell this story repeatedly. When we serve others by meeting their needs and healing their hurts, we are effective in connecting them with God. Visible love opens invisible hearts.

Serving is the highest level of meaningfulness for anyone's life. The meaning of life is easy to find if we simply serve others. A life without service is doomed to decay. "The great violinist Nicolo Paganini willed his marvellous violin to the city of his birth, Genoa, but only on the condition that the instrument never be played upon. It was an unfortunate condition, for it is a peculiarity of wood, that as long as it is used and handled, it shows little wear. As soon as it is discarded, it begins to decay. The exquisite, mellow-toned violin has become worm-eaten in its beautiful case, valueless except as a relic. The moldering instrument is a reminder that a life withdrawn from all service to others loses its meaning."[4]

Six Qualities of Servanthood

Let me identify six qualities of a servant demonstrated by Rebekah, the wife of Abraham's son Isaac. Rebekah lived a beautiful life of servanthood. She never dreamed how her serving heart would open the greatest doors of her life, but she discovered that serving opens doors of destiny.

1. Servanthood is willing.

"Drink, my lord," she said, and quickly lowered the jar to her hands and gave him a drink. After she had given him a drink, she said, "I'll draw water for your camels too, until they have finished drinking." So she quickly emptied her jar into the trough, ran back to the well to draw more water, and drew enough for all his camels.

Genesis 24:18-20 NIV

Rebekah doesn't complain that she has just been down at the well to get water for herself. She offers to get the man some water but she also offers to water his camels, even though the well was deep (around 50 steps would have descended to the water).

A camel can drink 25 gallons of water in one sitting. Ten camels make for the possibility of 250 gallons. Even if Rebekah had managed to carry five gallons up the steps each time, it could have taken her as many as 50 trips up and down the steps. Notwithstanding the effort required, she is keen! Unbeknown to Rebekah, this man, Eliezer, has just prayed that the woman who offers not just to satisfy his request for water but also to water his camels would be the woman destined for his master Abraham's son, Isaac.

Serving is an issue of the heart. Rebekah wanted to bless the man. She had no idea that there would be any reward for her efforts. Money can easily steal the heart. Once we receive money for what we once did freely from the heart, our willingness and enthusiasm can be compromised. In 1 Peter 5:2 Peter calls on us to serve the Lord with our hearts, not for money. Serving is its own pleasure. It is not motivated by any other reward.

Energy springs from willingness. Ask children to do something they don't want to, like clean their room, and nothing happens! They become like sloths—cute but slow. But tell them you're off to McDonalds and they're like streaked lightning, sitting in the car even before you finish the sentence. We are energised when our will is engaged. Fatigue follows the unwilling. We are tired when we're doing what we don't want to do. If we'd always rather be elsewhere, we'll never enjoy where we are right now. If we'd rather be doing something else, we won't have the energy or focus for what we're doing right now. Aligning our will and our action is basic to successful living.

The willing heart is:

- *Impelled rather than compelled.* Motivation comes from within rather than from some external pressure outside us. "People often say that motivation doesn't last. Well, neither does bathing; that's why we recommend it daily." (Zig Ziglar.)

- *Agreeable, not disagreeable.* We all think of the other point of view in a conversation, but we decide to focus on points of agreement rather than the points we disagree with. How painful is it when you're trying to hold a pleasant conversation with a disagreeable person? It's just hard work. The willing heart finds ways to agree and flow with people. Laurie Beth Jones says, "Agreeing to agree is a key to astonishing teamwork."[5]

- *Executing, not excusing.* The willing heart finds reasons to do, rather than reasons not to do. People with excuses reveal an unwilling attitude. Billy Sunday defined an excuse as "the skin of a reason stuffed with a lie." The person who is good at excuses is usually not good at anything else.

2. Servanthood excels.

Rebekah did the job well. She didn't half do the job. She finished what she started. In fact, she did more than was expected. Her service is surprising.

> *...when she had finished giving him a drink, she said, "I will draw water for your camels also, until they have finished drinking." Then she quickly emptied her pitcher into the trough, ran back to the well to draw water, and drew for all his camels.*
>
> Genesis 24:19-20

She makes sure the camels drink their fill. She doesn't just bring water until she feels she's done enough. She continues fetching water until the camels have had enough.

John F. Kennedy defined happiness as "the full use of your powers along lines of excellence."[6]

The servant from hell does the job only when it's convenient for them. They huff and puff, letting everyone know they're unhappy about doing it. They never do the job right or complete it properly. They complain about how much they've had to give up to do this. They tell you all the sacrifices they have made. They are going to do it for you, but they are determined to make you feel bad at the same time. When you see they're unhappy about doing it and offer to get it done some other way, they won't let it go: "No, no, I'll do it!" (heaving and sighing). Their service isn't coming free. Oh no! You're going to pay for it!

The true servant heart cannot do a job badly. They take pride in what they do and always do the best they can to surprise the person they're serving. Ask yourself this? "Are people surprised by what I do for them? Are they thankful? Do I bless them?"

Albert Einstein said, "We have to do the best we can. This is our sacred human responsibility."[7]

Rebekah sits among the matriarchal heads of Israel. History accepts her elevated station because her foundational lifestyle was self-less serving. Besides what the Bible reveals, we have to wonder how many other strangers she served joyfully as they passed by her well. Serving was a lifestyle to her, not just sporadic moments. Sometimes our teaching on servanthood sends a signal that if we are prepared to do menial tasks today (cleaning the lavatories is generally the task referred to), then one day we will graduate beyond serving. The fact is we never progress from serving. Even though I'm the senior minister of our church, I'll still clean up something right away if I can. It's not my job, but if I'm in a bathroom and the bowl needs cleaning, then I'll do it right then. I don't want the next person to come across a dirty bowl! Don't ever lose the heart that thinks about and serves others.

Martin Luther King, the great civil rights activist of the sixties, said, "If a man is called to be a street-sweeper, he should sweep streets even as Michelangelo painted, or as Beethoven composed music, or as Shakespeare wrote poetry. He should sweep streets so well that all the hosts of heaven and earth will pause and say, here lived a great street-sweeper who did his job well."[8]

3. Servanthood is swift.

True servants get the job done swiftly. Slow service is a curse worse than no service at all.

> ..."Drink, my lord," she said, and **quickly** lowered the jar to her hands and gave him a drink. ...she **quickly** emptied her jar into the trough, **ran** back to the well to draw more water...
>
> Genesis 24:18,20 NIV

Rebekah understood that speed is of the essence. Keeping people waiting is not serving at all. We surprise people with speed. And we actually deliver before it's due.

Jack Welch, former Chairman and CEO of General Electric, said this about Wal-Mart: "What Sam Walton did was to go into one of the most mature industries of all and find a way to make it grow, grow, grow, double-digit, month after month, year after year. He did it by innovation, customer focus, and above all, speed."[9]

Today, money is no longer the commodity people value most highly—time is! Taking more time from people than they are willing to give us incurs resentment and dissatisfaction. This is considered poor service. If we take less time than people anticipate, we win favor. How many times have you hung up the phone after the umpteenth transfer from one recorded message to another? How many times have you stepped out of a long line knowing that what you wanted is not worth the time it's going to take to get it? Find every way possible to reduce the amount of time it takes you to meet people's needs.

Geoff Alford, who for 20 years has conducted market research that specializes in customer satisfaction, says companies fail to understand that the components of customer service are timeliness, getting exactly what you ordered, getting it without hassles, and openness to feed-back if there are problems later on.[10]

Convenient servanthood doesn't exist. In fact, servanthood is nearly always going to be inconvenient. A servant serves at all times, not just when it is convenient.

> *"Which of you, having a servant plowing or tending sheep, will say to him when he has come in from the field, 'Come at once and sit down to eat'? But will he not rather say to him, 'Prepare something for my supper, and gird yourself and serve me till I have eaten and drunk, and afterward you will eat and drink'?"*
>
> Luke 17:7-8

4. Servanthood is honoring.

Servanthood honors rather than despises those it serves. Rebekah addresses the stranger as Sir.

> *So she said, "Drink, **my lord**." Then she quickly let her pitcher down to her hand, and gave him a drink.*
>
> Genesis 24:18

She treats the stranger with respect. Serving is serving. It is placing ourselves at the service of another. Serving is honoring and this is reflected in our language. We meet others' needs, not because we are some patronising do-gooder but because we respect people and use whatever we have to serve them.

Perhaps the Latvian chess master Aaron Nimzovich (1886-1935) underestimated the power of respect in the recipe for winning when he shouted to his victorious competitor, "How can I lose to such an idiot?"[11]

One of the most amazing churches in the world today is City Harvest Church in Singapore. Because of the close relationship Pastor Kong Hee and I have enjoyed over the years, we held our movement's first global conference in his great church. A large number of our staff members from Australia attended the conference. After the conference, I asked them to list the things they had learned from this church. Again and again people referred to the incredible servanthood of this beautiful congregation. The drummer in our band was floored when they addressed him as "Pastor" Brad and helped carry his bags.

People who are anxious about position find it impossible to serve. The servant heart is unconcerned about how we look to others. The most amazing person in history, Jesus Christ, demonstrated this time and again. Even though He is the immortal, sovereign, self-existing God of eternal spirit, He became a temporal, mortal, dependent man of flesh. Jesus, who for eternity had given commands, was now obeying them. He who had never committed a single wrong was condemned as an evildoer. He was crucified along with thieves, being the Lamb of God slain for the salvation of all people everywhere across all time. This is servanthood—not grasping to hold position.

Let this mind be in you, which was also in Christ Jesus, who, being in the form of God, did not consider it robbery to be equal with God, but made Himself of no reputation, taking the form of a bondservant, and coming in the likeness of men. And being found in appearance as a man, He humbled Himself and became obedient to the point of death, even the death of the cross.

Philippians 2:5-8

In Luke 14:8, Jesus tells us not to choose the most important seats at a function. He tells us not to seek to be the greatest but rather to be the least and take the lower seat. This means even though I might be a lead vocalist, if someone is needed in the choir, then I'm there. If pride prevents me from being involved at any level, then I just simply need to get involved and let pride die. Humility is something we do to ourselves—*"Humble yourselves..."* (James 4:10). We are all endeared to the humble. They are elevated in our eyes. Exaltation follows abasement.

5. Servanthood is work.

Serving is work. The servant attitude keeps working till the job is done. Some people work to fulfil a certain number of hours. The servant heart is there to get the job done, no matter how long it takes. Accomplishing the task overrides considerations of personal comfort.

*...she said, "I'll draw water for your camels too, **until they have finished drinking.**" So she quickly emptied her jar into the trough, ran back to the well to draw more water, and **drew enough for all his camels.***

Genesis 24:19-20 NIV

Of all the animals on earth, camels can be among the smelliest. They spit, snort, and are unusual beasts for a beautiful young woman to care for. Rebekah, however, was unconcerned. Her hospitality and her desire to serve overwhelmed any desire she might have had for personal comfort. She would do whatever it took to bless this foreigner asking to drink at their well. Hospitality is the love of strangers. It's one thing to welcome, bless, and serve people we know, but to do the same for complete strangers—that's different.

Rebekah was "Miss Hospitality." The well would have been serviced by a flight of around 50 steps spiralling against the wall down to the water. A camel can drink up to 25 gallons of water at one sitting. Eliezer had ten camels. They were carrying a large cargo, so they were thirsting for their 25-gallon drink. What was Rebekah thinking! This is one different kind of lady! Getting Eliezer his cup of water was nothing compared to what she was now offering. He accepted her offer. This meant her making 50 trips up and down the steps, carrying five gallons up from the well each time.

This is a servant's heart. Rebekah didn't realize it but this was her doorway to destiny. Once she had finished, Eliezer knew his prayer had been answered. He had prayed that the woman who not only gave him a drink but also offered to water his camels would be the one God had chosen for his master Abraham's son, Isaac. He opened the treasure chests from the camels' backs and began showering the young woman with jewelery and gifts. He asked her if she would be prepared to travel back to his land with him and marry his master's son.

As the story unfolds, it is obvious to Rebekah that God's great hand has been guiding this incredible sequence of events. She agrees and returns with Eliezer. The moment she meets Isaac, they fall in love. They become central figures in the amazing tapestry of God's purpose of bringing the Messiah into our world.

Let me share one of the most graphic illustrations I know of regarding the power of servanthood opening the doors of destiny. One stormy night many years ago, an elderly man and his wife entered the lobby of a small hotel in Philadelphia. Trying to get out of the rain, the couple approached the front desk hoping to get some shelter for the night. "Could you possibly give us a room here?" the husband asked.

The clerk, a friendly man with a winning smile, looked at the couple and explained that there were three conventions in town. "All of our rooms are taken," the clerk said. "But I can't send a nice couple like you out into the rain at one o'clock in the morning. Would you perhaps be willing to sleep in my room? It's not exactly a suite, but it will be good enough to make you folks comfortable for the night." When the couple declined, the young man pressed on. "Don't worry about me. I'll make out just fine," he assured them. So the couple agreed.

As he paid his bill the next morning, the elderly man said to the clerk, "You are the kind of manager who should be the boss of the best hotel in the United States. Maybe one day I'll build one for you."

The clerk looked at them and smiled. The three of them had a good laugh. As they drove away, the elderly couple agreed that the helpful clerk was indeed exceptional. It wasn't easy to find people who were both friendly and helpful.

Two years passed. The clerk had almost forgotten the incident when he received a letter from the old man. It recalled the stormy night and enclosed a round-trip ticket to New York, asking the young man to pay them a visit.

The old man met him in New York and led him to the corner of Fifth Avenue and 34th Street. He pointed to a great new building there, a palace of reddish stone with turrets and watchtowers thrusting up to the sky. "That," said the old man, "is the hotel I have just built for you to manage."

"You must be joking!" the young man said.

"I can assure you I am not," replied the old man, a sly smile playing around his mouth. The old man's name was William Waldorf Astor, and the magnificent structure was the original Waldorf-Astoria Hotel. The young clerk who became its first manager was George C. Boldt[12].

The servant does whatever it takes to get the job done. Servanthood opens the door to the fulfilment of promises.

Abraham was one of the wealthiest men of his day. Yet this man of amazing wealth and power also understood the nature of serving:

> *Then the Lord appeared to him by the terebinth trees of Mamre, as he was sitting in the tent door in the heat of the day.*
>
> Genesis 18:1

It was a hot day and the hottest time of the day—not the most convenient time to be running around looking after people when you have servants by the dozen to do it for you. Abraham was relaxing. He had just sat down.

> *So he lifted his eyes and looked, and behold, three men were standing by him; and when he saw them, he ran from the tent door to meet them, and bowed himself to the ground....*
>
> Genesis 18:2

When Abraham sees the three men, he doesn't groan, he doesn't moan—he runs. He is eager and willing. He bows low. (Remember, this is Abraham, one of the wealthiest men on earth.) He establishes very quickly that he is there to serve them, with honor.

> *...and said, "My Lord, if I have now found favor in Your sight, do not pass on by Your servant."*
>
> Genesis 18:3

He considers it a privilege to serve them. He doesn't simply presume that they will accept his hospitality.

"Please let a little water be brought, and wash your feet, and rest yourselves under the tree."

Genesis 18:4

He gives some thought as to what they might like, not just what he would like to do for them. Having your feet washed and being allowed to sit in the shade is exactly what any traveller would appreciate the most.

"I will bring a morsel of bread, that you may refresh your hearts. After that you may pass by, inasmuch as you have come to your servant." They said, "Do as you have said."'

Genesis 18:5

Abraham doesn't boast that he will put on a large feast, even though that is exactly what he is planning to do. He isn't asking anything more of them than that they let him serve them, then feel free to pass on by. He doesn't tell them that he is then going to show them some home movies, or take them on a tour of his favorite camel trails, or ask them to carry some presents for him to distant desert friends.

Abraham hurried into the tent to Sarah and said, "Quickly, make ready three measures of fine meal; knead it and make cakes." And Abraham ran to the herd, took a tender and good calf, gave it to a young man, and he hastened to prepare it. So he took butter and milk and the calf, which he had prepared, and set it before them; and he stood by them under the tree as they ate.

Genesis 18:6-8

He doesn't eat with them in order to devote himself to serving them. He becomes their waiter, making sure he is ready to meet any need they may have.

> *Then they said to him, "Where is Sarah your wife?" So he said, "Here, in the tent." And He said, "I will certainly return to you according to the time of life, and behold, Sarah your wife shall have a son." (Sarah was listening in the tent door which was behind him.)*
>
> Genesis 18:9-10

Once again we see servanthood opening doors of destiny. Because Abraham humbled himself and served these people (not realizing that it was actually God who had decided to pay him a visit), the Lord promised him a child. Abraham had desired this all his life and now God was going to fulfil the prayer. Hospitality and servanthood secured the result Abraham had ached for all his life.

6. Servanthood is unselfish.

Rebekah had other people's interests at heart. So did Paul's disciple, Timothy. The apostle speaks about Timothy as a son who serves.

> *I have no one like-minded, who will sincerely care for your state. For all seek their own, not the things which are of Christ Jesus.*
>
> Philippians 2:20-21

Sadly, Paul's words are true: I have no one who will sincerely care for you. Few people are enough interested in others that they will go out of their way to satisfy others' needs. People we employ will mostly do just what they are employed to do. Beyond that, their own priorities are their primary pursuits. But when people's work becomes their passion, the sacrifices serving demands are hardly noticed.

Selfishness is defined as "stinginess resulting from a concern for your own welfare and a disregard of others."[13]

If I expect professionals such as accountants and lawyers to do all the creative thinking regarding my business, I'll be disappointed. What I do is tell them the result I want and ask them to tell me how to get there. I offer some of my own ideas as well. "Can't we do this or that?" Even if I'm told I can't, I'll get another opinion from elsewhere.

If I tell the maitre d' of a restaurant that my wife and I are celebrating our wedding anniversary, I'll ask for a table near a window or near the fireplace or with the best view, not in the middle of the room or near the kitchen or the toilet doors. If I don't say exactly what I want and what I don't want, too often we'll end up being placed exactly where we didn't want to be. It's rare to find others thinking for you. We assume they are but mostly they're not. This is where a Christian can shine—in thinking about other people's wishes, in anticipating, and meeting their desires. This is practical love in action.

I've found that most architects are happy to use my money to build their building rather than try and build the one I want. This may sound cynical but it's not. It is simply realizing that we are naive to imagine that people will generally be thinking of how they can best serve us and make our lives more pleasant. Most people are looking out for themselves.

Even when you do find a servant-hearted person, they still generally need to be told what is needed. This is the difference between a servant and a son. A son has the seed of the father, or the spirit of the father within. In that spirit, he takes the initiative to look after the needs of the father.

Paul says he has found in Timothy one young man who is a son, who has Paul's interests at heart. Because of that, Timothy also carries the care of the churches, just as Paul does (see 2 Cor. 11:28).

The most valuable people are those who serve. That's why they receive the recognition and opportunities others would like but don't receive because their selfishness overrides their usefulness.

So here ends the lesson from Rebekah, the servant hero for all of us everywhere.

The New Testament also abounds with men and women who discovered the spirit of servanthood. Among the long list of those who worked with and served Paul is Epaphroditus, who risked his life in the call:

> Yet I considered it necessary to send to you Epaphroditus, my brother, fellow worker, and fellow soldier, but your messenger and the one who ministered to my need; since he was longing for you all, and was distressed because you had heard that he was sick. For indeed he was sick almost unto death; but God had mercy on him, and not only on him but on me also, lest I should have sorrow upon sorrow. Therefore I sent him the more eagerly, that when you see him again you may rejoice, and I may be less sorrowful. Receive him therefore in the Lord with all gladness, and hold such men in esteem; because for the work of Christ he came close to death, not regarding his life, to supply what was lacking in your service toward me.'
>
> Philippians 2:25-30

Epaphroditus is a name associated with the goddess of gambling. Paul plays on the word when he refers to the man risking (gambling) his life for God. This man had gambled his life for the sake of serving God. In the same way, during the plague in 252 A.D., the Christian Bishop, Cyprian, led the early Christians of Carthage to bury the dead and nurse the sick in the stricken city when bodies were thrown into the streets. There was a group called the *"paraboloni"* (the gamblers) who visited prisoners and the sick, especially those who were dangerous or who had highly infectious diseases.

Epaphroditus had braved the wild seas that stormed at that time of year, the treacherous back roads to Rome, and the danger of being associated with Paul, the man charged with treason. He moved into the prison to be a servant to Paul in his suffering, as there were little or no provisions, food, clothing, or bedding for prisoners.

Paul was moved to write by the need of the church to be comforted. They loved Epaphroditus so much they had become distressed when they heard he was sick. Paul was aching to visit the Philippian church.

Paul calls Epaphroditus brother, fellow worker, fellow soldier, messenger, and minister.

Brother: This implies he has the same father, and therefore carries the same genetics, the same instincts.

Fellow worker: Epaphroditus is not a "consumer" Christian but a "producer" Christian. Paul says that just as he worked, so did Epaphroditus. This is about being useful and proving our worth.

Our fellowship is in working together.

Fellow soldier: This is a man who fights the good fight. When I fight, so does he. Our fellowship is in that we are fighting the same fight. He covers me when I need it, and I cover him when he needs it.

Messenger: Paul is saying that Epaphroditus can be trusted with carrying my message, not his own. I can trust him to take gifts I am giving to others.

Minister: He ministers to me and to others so they are impacted, transformed, touched, and blessed.

2

SON OF A GUN

It is impossible to build a great church without a team of amazing people. I'm not just talking about those we call the ministry team, eldership, or leaders. I'm referring to everyone in the church. Every single person in the body is gifted and called. Everyone has a place in the body. Our purpose as a believer is discovered as we do whatever it is we are called to do. The context of our calling is the church in which we are members.

> *I trust in the Lord Jesus to send Timothy to you shortly, that I also may be encouraged when I know your state. For I have no one like-minded, who will sincerely care for your state. For all seek their own, not the things which are of Christ Jesus. But you know his proven character, that as a son with his father he served with me in the gospel.*
>
> Philippians 2:19-22

Paul wrote this letter in response to the gifts the Philippians had sent to him while he was in prison. (The prison didn't provide any food or supplies for the inmates—all this came from family and friends).

27

Sons Bear the Genetic Code of the House

The King James Version says Timothy would naturally care for the well being of the Philippians because he was likeminded. The New American Standard Bible uses the term "kindred spirit." Even though he is not his natural offspring, Paul calls Timothy his son. Timothy has the same spirit. He is likeminded. He will naturally and instinctively care for the Philippians just as Paul would. As a son, he embraces the culture of his "father," Paul. He instinctively knows the "ways" of Paul. Amazingly, the apostle says he had no one else like this. Servants and soldiers are comparatively easy to find. Sons, however, are rare. Sons differ from servants in that they know what the father would want. They share his heart. A servant needs to be told what to do. A son who serves knows what to do to carry out the plans of the father without being told.

Paul reveals that sons are rare because "all seek their own." When our hearts are self-oriented, we cannot embrace another's heart. When we die to ourselves, we are able to feel the heart of another and use our lives to accomplish their purpose. This is sonship.

Timothy didn't come to Christ through Paul, nor was he raised in a church that Paul pastored. He became a son by choice, by adoption. Even though their backgrounds were extremely different, Paul treated him as a son and Timothy accepted Paul as a father. Timothy was born of a Greek father and a Jewish mother, Eunice. His grandmother Lois met Paul on his second missionary journey. The apostle saw the great potential in Timothy.

Paul and Timothy became close during the many adventures they shared in Paul's journeys. They travelled together to Philippi. Timothy was with Paul in Berea, Thessalonica, Corinth, and Ephesus. He was then in prison with him in Rome. He helped Paul write five of his letters. The book of Hebrews reveals that in the end Timothy also became a prisoner for Christ, most likely because he was close to Paul. Timothy's great usefulness was that he was prepared to do anything, go anywhere, be servant or leader—anything at all to fulfil the vision God had required Paul to accomplish.

People become sons and daughters either by birth or by adoption. When God brings us into His family, it is through birth *and* adoption. Adoption is a two-way street. We adopt a child but the child must also adopt us. This also applies to the particular church we find ourselves placed in. We become part of that local family. We become a son or daughter of that house either through being born again there or by being adopted into that house. We imbibe the spirit of the house.

That this will happen, however, is not guaranteed. If we fall short of becoming baptised into the spirit of the house, then we are sons and daughters in name only. Some offspring never embrace the spirit, values, or ways of their natural family. Others are adopted and fully become sons or daughters by totally embracing all of the spirit and culture of the house.

My experience is that even when people are born again under your ministry and in your house, that is still no guarantee that they will become sons and daughters of the house. It greatly increases the likelihood, but it isn't the only element of a genetic download. This actually happens in a moment of correction, discipline, or adjustment. We need adjustment only in areas in which we are wrong, so it can be a difficult moment. Hebrews says chastising is never pleasant. However, the writer also says if we are not partakers of correction, we are not sons but illegitimate (see Heb. 12:8). We might bear the name and the heritage but not the spirit. If we are smart, we will correct ourselves.

Taking it upon ourselves relieves us of the challenge that comes when another corrects us. We also learn one of the most important lessons anyone can learn—that is, the ability to learn, to be self-taught. If we judge ourselves, we won't need to be judged! (see 1 Cor. 11:31).

Lot's flocks and herds had increased so much that there was strife between him and his Uncle Abraham's servants in competing for grasslands. This should never have happened. Lot was obviously building his house under the blessing of Abraham. If he were wise, he would have built Abraham's house and continued to receive blessing by virtue of living so close to the man. Instead, he allows the strife to rise until Abraham asks him to separate, offering Lot first choice of location. Again, Lot should have replied that it wasn't for him to choose. He should either have given his uncle leave to tell him where to go or allowed Abraham to choose first and then take whatever was left.

The Scripture tells us that *"Lot chose for himself..."* (Gen. 13:11). This will always be a poor decision. We need to live for something bigger than ourselves so that our choices are for God, for others, or for a great cause, but certainly not just for our own paltry kingdom. Lot had the position of a ruler but he exercised poor, weak, and damaging leadership. Characteristics of poor leadership are not difficult to find in Lot:

- Selfish decisions (Gen. 13:11).
- Getting without giving (Gen. 13:11).
- Choices based on desires of the flesh rather than desires of the spirit (Gen. 13:10).
- Easily compromised convictions. (Gen. 13:12-13).

- Feeling conviction but failing to act; vexed but unchanging (2 Pet. 2:8).

- Lacking credibility and authority with his own family.

- Laughed at when he warns of impending judgment (Gen. 19:14).

- A wife reluctant to leave Sodom (Gen. 19:26).

- Giving birth to problems, not answers—his daughters make him drunk so they can have sex with him to have their own children (Gen. 19:30-36).

- Always needing rescuing (Gen. 14:16; 19:10,16).

Even though for years Abraham's nephew Lot travelled close to the great Patriarch of the Hebrew nation, he never caught the spirit of the man. He partook of the blessings of Abraham but never acquired the roots of the blessing. He didn't embrace the character of the man of God, his walk with God, his self-sacrificing obedience to God, his family life, or his faith. And yet, 318 servants born in Abraham's house, although not related to him, did actually imbibe the genetics of Abraham's spirituality (see Gen. 14:14). They fought alongside Abraham, defeating a confederation of four kingdoms that had wiped out king after king in a rampage across the land. Genesis reveals Abraham not only as a man of faith and obedience and as the friend of God, but also as a man of war. He possessed courage combined with brilliant strategy to recover all that these kings had plundered from Sodom and Gomorrah. In rescuing Lot, Abraham also rescued all those others who had been captured from Sodom and Gomorrah.

Sons Serve the Vision of the House

A son who serves evidences proven character. This is not just about being a son but rather a son who serves. The *New American Standard Bible* calls it proven worth (see Phil. 2:22). Our worth is proven in serving as sons.

Timothy bought into the spiritual genetics of Paul, who says he has no one else like Timothy. He was like-minded. He instinctively cared for the people the same way Paul cared for them. Others failed to share Paul's spirit because their self-interest exceeded their interest in Christ. Their ministry was for their own benefit more than for others. Such people gather and build a congregation because it serves their own purpose. This is the difference between self-serving leadership and people-serving leadership.

Paul's disciples were great workers but some had parted from him, while others had even turned on him. "Proving" worth discovers true character under pressure. Serving develops character. Serving as a son interprets a father's dream and then makes it happen.

Sons Share Pride in Their House

When I was young, as far as I was concerned our house was the best in town. I was always proud to bring friends home. Sons love welcoming friends into their home. Sons share a pride in their house. They ensure the house is a great place to be. They repair, clean, and keep their house looking good.

Sons take pride in their father, their mother, their brothers and sisters, and friends of the house. Fathers take pride in their children. Their boast is their family.

Children's children are the crown of old men, and the glory of children is their father.

Proverbs 17:6

The way we see our church deeply affects levels of growth. If we are embarrassed about our church, we won't bring anyone along. I know many believers who feel better about our church than they feel about the church they go to, so they bring their unchurched friends to our church rather than to their own. How sad is that!

If the self-image of the leader is good, the self-image of the church will also be good. The leader's mission is to ensure that his people feel great about their church. The successful leader works hard to make every area a reason for healthy pride.

Exceeding expectations always upgrades self-image. People who go the second mile feel great that they have done it, and those surprised by the exceptional treatment will shout it from the housetops. Second-mile service means being more generous than you want to be. It means excellence. It means caring for people extraordinarily well. It means worship that creates a sense of awe, preaching that leaves people excited with inspiration, messages that turn people's worlds around. The organization is dramatic. The hospitality is five-star plus.

Sons Accept Discipline in Their House

...My son, do not despise the chastening of the Lord, nor be discouraged when you are rebuked by Him; For whom the Lord loves He chastens, and scourges every son whom He receives.

If you endure chastening, God deals with you as with sons; for what son is there whom a father does not chasten?...Now no chastening seems to be joyful for the present, but painful; nevertheless, afterward it yields the peaceable fruit of righteousness to those who have been trained by it.

Therefore strengthen the hands which hang down, and the feeble knees, and make straight paths for your feet, so that what is lame may not be dislocated, but rather be healed.

Hebrews 12:5-7,11-13

A true son receives correction with a teachable attitude. Chastising forms character in us like nothing else can.

In receiving chastising remember:

- You will be rewarded after the chastising (James 1:2-4).

- It will not go on forever. It will finish (see 1 Cor. 10:13).

- Your trial is the doorway to your next stage (see Ps. 105:19-22).

- God will deliver you out of the trial (see Ps. 34:19).

- The rebuke will not be more than you can bear (see 1 Cor. 10:13).

God desires a broken and a contrite spirit (see Ps. 51:17). The power of our spirit remains hidden until broken. Mary broke a flask of scented oil over Jesus. The fragrance permeated the entire house (see Luke 7:37-38). Watchman Nee suggests that we are like the flask. The fragrance of Christ effuses from us after we have travelled through events that break us open to God.[1]As long as we remain unbroken, Christ remains locked within. Emerging from trials with softened hearts, however, the character of Christ flows easily. We are not white-knuckling it, trying to be like Christ. It comes naturally.

The fire also purifies our worship. To prepare for the call of God many of us go to Bible college, but under the surface He sends us to the furnace. We study the ways of success in seminars, but behind the scenes, God lays us on His anvil. His hammer shapes us into the person He can use. We seek mentors to develop us. Meanwhile, the Potter shapes us on His wheel.

Passing through such times, our character develops in the same way a son matures. I know people I could help today if they would simply hear me. Not as someone with the optional message of a life coach, but as a father. My message would be challenging but I know it could save them. Even though they are serving the Lord, they have not become sons or daughters of the house. If I were really to speak to them about those sensitive issues they need to hear about and that could transform their lives, their reaction would be unpredictable. As I've seen some do, they might leave, taking all their baggage with them. I try to gauge whether a person has really become a son of the house, whether their purpose is the purpose of the house or their own agenda. This tells me at what level I can speak to them.

Sons Give Birth to Sons

Whatever we are is what we'll reproduce. None of us is without influence. Our lives are a message to others. Our attitude is contagious. People with a son-of-the-house attitude cause others to have the same. I don't have to drill into the center of a tree's trunk to discover its quality. I need only to see the fruit. This is why Paul used Timothy extensively. He wanted others to get the same spirit that Timothy had. Sons bring people not only to God but also to His house, the house they are sons in. The people they influence become immersed not only in God; they are also immersed into the house. Those who are grounded in church have a far greater chance of remaining grounded in God.

3

SOLDIER THROUGH AND THROUGH

The church grows in a climate of war.

...I will build My church, and the gates of Hades shall not prevail against it.

Matthew 16:18

The word *church*(from the Greek *ecclesia*) means "called out ones." The term is borrowed from the description of Roman citizens who, although they lived in lands distant from Italy, were nonetheless distinguished from the local peoples. They had rights and preferences that were unavailable to the people of the occupied nations. The Roman Empire was conquering the world and expanding on all fronts. It seemed no nation could resist the force of the great Roman armies conquering one army after another.

At the same time, they also brought many improvements and benefits to those nations. They built roads and highways, aqueducts offering reliable water supplies even in droughts, harbours, gardens, baths, bridges, and magnificent architecture of amphitheatres, theatres, temples, porticos, and triumphal arches. The local worlds of the conquered nations often improved, even though it was at the price of independence. The historian Edward Gibbon notes that the governing Roman presence was not always despised; in fact it was sometimes even welcomed: "The vanquished nations...resigned the hope, nay even the wish of resuming their independence."[1]

This point is vital to note. When Jesus declared He would build His *ecclesia,* His disciples would immediately have thought of the rapid, powerful expansion of the Roman Empire and the fact that even though in Palestine the Romans were despised (mostly because of their defiling idol worship), it was commonly accepted that wherever the Roman presence ruled, it had mostly upgraded life. Jesus anticipated that not only would His church conquer wherever the devil ruled, but it would also upgrade life for those accepting His rule in their lives.

Jesus says the gates of hell will fail in trying to withstand His advancing church. Gates refer to the political and commercial nerve center of an ancient Middle Eastern city. The leaders governed from the city gates. This is where the powerful people around town would gather. The most impacting decisions were made here. Kings went to war from the gates.

Jesus uses the metaphor of gates so that we understand what we are confronting. He is saying that all the powers of hell combined are no match for the onslaught of the church. Understand that He is not saying we are holding out against the onslaught of hell. Hell is unable to defend itself against the onslaught of the church. The Parliament House of hell, the White House of hell, the Pentagon of hell, the Downing Street of hell—all are unable to prevail against the church of Jesus Christ. This picture is very different to the perception most of us have had. We sometimes feel that we are holding out against the attack of hell. We often hear it said that we are under attack. But Jesus declares this is not how it is meant to be. We are the invaders. Hell's defenses are powerless against the might of the church. Our weapons bind the strong man (Mark 3:27) and plunder hell. Jesus' church expands by conquering hearts and vanquishing demons throughout the earth.

As with any war, victory rests with those who lead and those who fight. Jesus announces that He will build His church, and that He will build it on those who have insight into who He is and who they themselves are. Peter was destined to be a great leader in the early church but with fledgling leadership qualities that needed to be developed. Much of this took place as he battled with demons, his own frailties, and high-pressure circumstances. Peter came under the influence of demons, urging Christ to deflect from His course. He battled defeat when his faith failed him and he sank in the ocean. His fear of people's opinions crippled his witness when he denied he had any connection with Christ (see Matt. 16:23, 14:30; John 18:17).

Following Christ involves difficult times. Sometimes war surrounds us. We find ourselves in difficulties from behind, from in front, from above, from below, from the left, and from the right. Accepting this fact arms us with a mind that helps assure victory (see 1 Peter 4:1). We are in a war. We are soldiers. It's part of the call upon us. We may not all be enlisted in our national military, but once we receive Christ, like it or not, we are unquestionably enlisted in the army of God. Who wins wars? These are the people Jesus builds on. These are the leaders in His kingdom, His church.

Soldiers Are Strong

...endure hardship as a good soldier of Jesus Christ.

2 Timothy 2:3

The late Dr. Ed Cole declared, "In these tough times, the world is crying out for strong men. It needs men who can overcome drifting philosophies and restore order, hope, dignity and heroic action."[2]

Tough times can threaten to overwhelm us but the strong endure pressure. Not only do they endure, they turn the situation around. Leaders are strong. Discovering where their strength lies is imperative. Even in our weaknesses we can become strong through Christ.

As Moses prepares to resign from leading Israel, his successor Joshua is told by three different sources to be strong as he becomes the leader. Even though he has been a soldier all his life, he has also been a servant, attending to the great man of God, Moses. These two roles have forged the character of the man who is to take Israel into their Promised Land. At this stage, however, God is commanding the man to be strong (see Josh. 1:6). Moses had also told him to be strong (see Deut. 31:7). And all Israel exhorts him to be strong (see Josh. 1:18). Strength is not optional but rather imperative in leaders. People will not follow weak, uncourageous leaders. They line up behind the courageous, the strong, the warriors.

During the Nazi air raids on London in World War II, the people of London scattered for the bomb shelters. But Winston Churchill went to the rooftop and railed into the night sky against Hitler, promising to defeat him.

The leader is settled on the fact that life is a war. Occasionally I've found myself complaining, feeling weary from the fight. The only response I hear from the Lord is, "Get used to it!" You and I have to accept that warfare is intrinsic to the life of the leader. This is how we avoid Bunyan's pilgrim's "Slough of Despond."

The strength of a soldier shines when others are retreating and avoiding the confrontation. As the leader, you know there is nothing else to do except face the enemy. One of the great scenes in the movie *The Patriot* is when the leader-warrior, played by Mel Gibson, sees his ragtag militia retreating back over the hill. He lays hold of the flag and begins racing to the crest, running through the troops in the opposite direction toward the enemy. At the sight of just one brave soldier refusing defeat, the militia rise with fresh courage. They turn and rush the enemy and secure victory.

The strength of a soldier is tested most under the temptation to compromise. Temptation will always be more intense upon the leader than those they lead. The devil is well aware that if the shepherd is struck, the sheep are scattered. (see Zech. 13:7). John Bevere relates the story of an occasion when his wife was sitting next to a person on a plane who declined the in-flight meal. Because he was fasting, she assumed he was a Christian and asked him. He replied, "I'm not a Christian. I'm a Satanist. We're fasting against Christian leaders and their marriages. We're praying for them to fall into adultery." We are engaged in a deadly struggle with demons that are scheming to drag us away from our purpose and into darkness. But even though these battles rage, the leader-warrior knows how to defeat demons, resisting temptation, and the devil, overpowering the enemy with the mighty weapons God has given us.

Our strength is clearly revealed as the pressures of leadership increase. The measure of stress we can live with is the measure of our strength. Physically strong people can carry physically heavy loads. Strong leaders carry the burden of their leadership without collapsing. Our need is not for greater understanding of the pressure but for more strength. Without strength, the leader loses patience under pressure.

They lose joy facing the impossible. They become fearful and under attack. None of us are equal to the call God places upon us, so we need to gain strength from the strong. We need to wait on the Lord.

...be strong in the Lord and in the power of His might.

Ephesians 6:10

Soldiers Are Obedient

Success in war rests with each soldier carrying out orders.

A soldier must be able to take orders. Of all the disciplines a soldier must learn, the basic one is obedience. They must accept authority. They must accept obedience.

Obey those who rule over you....

Hebrews 13:17

This is not calling leaders to assume rulership over us. Rather, it's calling us to place ourselves in obedience to our leaders.

When God gave the Ten Commandments to Moses, they were not the "Ten Suggestions." When God gives a command, it is to be obeyed, not weighed. Obedience is not a popular word in our independent, free culture. There may be times we don't understand the why of the commands of Scripture. But we obey rather than second-guess the commands of God.

The calamitous demise of King Saul is described in 1 Samuel 13. As Israel exited Egypt led by Moses, the desert tribe of Amalek attacked Israel from the rear where all the children, the weak, the aged, and the sick would travel (see Deut. 25:18). God would not let this savage and cowardly war strategy pass without recompense. Saul's reign was the time when Jehovah had purposed to execute judgment upon Amalek. King Saul was His agent of execution. Our leadership is based on doing not what we think but on what God tells us, even when we don't understand why. The judgment on Amalek was exactly what their design had been on Israel when they were escaping from Egypt. This knowledge and the depth of feeling God had for this justice escaped Saul's comprehension.

Saul was not guided by a voice from above or an impression within. It was a man, the prophet Samuel. God guides, leads, and commands us through influencers He places in our lives.

Our Christian world seems to encourage people to seek supernatural inspiration and experiences. These are amazing when they're authentic. But these impressions can fall easily into being employed to justify avoiding obedience. Sometimes we want some things more than the will of God. We are clever at cloaking these desires with the line "God told me."

Some time ago, my wife Christine was approached by a young lady in one of our services wanting a "word" from the Lord. Chris asked her if she came to our church. She didn't. Asking what the issue was, she explained to Chris that she wanted to marry a certain young man. Chris asked if she had talked with her pastor at her own church. She said she had but that the pastor didn't agree with their plans. Chris said to her, "Here's the word of the Lord—listen to your pastor."

Gifts of the Spirit, personal revelation, visions, and voices do not supersede or substitute for the Bible. Supernatural experiences serve to confirm what is written in the Word of God.

Soldiers Are Disciplined

Among other things, discipline is doing what you do not want to do. Discipline is also not doing something you want to do. Discipline is consistently doing the things you should do. Discipline is the making of character, indiscipline the unmaking of character. Doing something repeatedly creates a habit, a way of life. Our habits form our lives, good or bad.

The world lies at the feet of the disciplined person. Some imagine the race is won by the talented, the intelligent, the gifted, the well connected. However, medals never rest on the chest of the undisciplined.

Samuel Taylor Coleridge was a living example of how immense talent can be squandered on the altar of indolence. William Barclay said of him,

> Coleridge is the supreme tragedy of indiscipline. Never did so great a mind produce so little. He left Cambridge University to join the army; he left the army because he could not rub down a horse; he returned to Oxford and left without a degree. Coleridge had every poetic gift but one—the gift of sustained and concentrated effort.[3]

Discipline's choice is a life lived by principles rather than by feelings. Discipline has already decided how she will live, well before meeting the fork in the road. Her choices have already been made. There is no pondering. Successful personal government demands adherence to values we've already committed to.

The king maker and historian Samuel records the tragic tale of a young prince ruining his life with unrestrained lust, plummeting his future and his entire family into sorrow after sorrow (see 2 Sam. 13). Amnon, a son of King David, is deeply obsessed with someone he shouldn't be—his sister Tamar. Infatuation floods reason from his mind. He grows ill with obsession. He schemes to capture her alone in his bedroom and rape her. When he succeeds, however, his "love" suddenly changes to violent disgust. He throws her out of his room. Her disgrace is complete. Tamar's incensed brother Absalom exacts fatal revenge, killing Amnon two years later.

One sorry moment of unrestrained lust rained disaster not only on Amnon himself but also on all those around him. As a king's son, Amnon was destined for leadership. An essential of leadership is discipline. This was his great opportunity to learn it. He could have grown that strength of character fitting for great leadership by overruling his own immense passions. Instead, however, he fell to the temptation. He forfeited all.

The torment of resisting temptation, although tortuously difficult, is far less tormenting than the consequences of yielding to it. Our heart is in the hand of our will. Even love and forgiveness can be summoned through choice. The widespread and deeply popular concept that we fall in love or find love leaves us in an extremely unpredictable emotional state. This may happen occasionally, but the norm we need to expect is that we are responsible to love through choice. The top two commandments Moses delivered and Jesus confirmed are to love God and to love one another. They are commands, not suggestions, not happenstances. Our God has issued commands that He is fully aware we can obey. That's why we make the vow at the marriage altar. We vow to love our spouse. Deep chemistry and love brings us to the point of marriage, but that strength of feeling is not going to survive every day. We need to decide to love even when we don't want to. We declare that we choose to love. In fact, we vow to God to love our spouse. So we love the person we are meant to love in the way we're meant to love them by the choices of our heart.

In the absence of premade choices, we're at the mercy of our emotions, which were never meant to rule us but rather to serve us. Deep-fried battered fish and chips smell far better *before* we eat them than they feel *after* we have eaten them. Likewise, sin looks, smells, and fantasizes better before we do it than afterwards when self-disgust, self-loathing, self-hatred, and disappointment take over. Like Amnon, we find ourselves destroying the most important relationships around us because we let emotions rather than principles rule us.

Governing ourselves means gaining mastery over our motivations, attitudes, thoughts, and actions. We adhere to predetermined decisions, rather than scramble to make them in the moment. We fix these decisions in the clear-minded space of zero pressure. For example, smart people will tell you to decide what your financial limit is before you go to an auction. Unarmed with this decision, you risk losing your reason in the heat of bidding. Then you're left facing the agony of an impossible stretch to fulfil the bid. The auction is like our lives. We need to set our boundaries before we meet the situations that test them.

Soldiers Are Devoted

No one engaged in warfare entangles himself with the affairs of this life, that he may please him who enlisted him as a soldier.

2 Timothy 2:4

The word *warfare* means "to be engaged in a military campaign." The other keyword in this passage is *entangle,* which means "to in weave." Our focus blurs with an inweaving, entwining world, distracting our loves and desires from God. What the heart loves, the mind dwells on. Warfare demands single-minded, totally committed, undistracted focus. If our minds are focused on money, relationships, or possessions, we are blind to the enemy's advance. Preoccupied elsewhere, we are easily taken advantage of.

The leader-soldier is focused. Our focus fixes on what matters. Surprisingly, the issue is not so much focusing on the right things, but rather on not becoming distracted by the wrong things. There are a thousand and one things we can give ourselves to, but there will be one thing above all others that we must devote our attention to. We can't do everything. We are not called to do everything. We shouldn't attempt to do everything.

Soldiers Are Awake

Leadership is a war zone. Occupying the leader's seat, you're immediately in the crosshairs of the enemy. The principle is clear: Strike the shepherd, scatter the sheep (see Zech. 13:7). With tragic consistency, we hear of leaders struck down again and again. This war is ferocious. The casualties are neither small nor insignificant. Every time another leader falls, thousands are affected.

In my early days of church leadership, I complained to God about this unrelenting warfare. I would just manage to surmount one problem when another would arrive. And sometimes not just one, but a multitude. If I gained victory on my right hand, another challenge would rise on the left. God replied, "Get used to it. This is your life from here on." There was no choice. I settled into the harness of a soldier. This soldier's mind-set equips us for the unremitting war every effective leader inevitably faces.

This preparedness, however, is not all we need for victory. Intelligence regarding the tactics of the devil is also essential. As Paul says, "...*we are not ignorant of his devices*" (2 Cor. 2:11). The devices of the devil are not just bad behavior in people. This misreading is an ignorance Satan employs to camouflage his schemes. The apostle enlightens us, however, by explaining that "...*we are not fighting against people made of flesh and blood, but against...wicked spirits in the spirit world*"(Eph. 6:12 NLT). For example, when you're on the receiving end of destructive, depressing criticism, it's easy to pass it off as just people being people. But we need to realize that the source of condemnation is not people but the accuser of the brethren, the devil (see Rev. 12:10). When strife storms our homes, we can think it is just family members being angry at each other. But the devil is the source of strife. His intent is to destroy relationships. If your heart becomes infatuated with someone other than your spouse, this temptation is from the devil. He aims to destroy our integrity and subsequently our lives.

The devil accuses, slanders, backbites, gossips, and criticizes (see Rev. 12:10); he tempts with sin (see Matt. 4:3); he hinders the gospel (see 1 Thess. 2:18); he steals the Word of God from the heart (see Mark 4:15); he persecutes, opposes, and slanders Christians (see Zech. 3:1,2); he blinds people's minds to the gospel (see 2 Cor. 4:4); he tries to hinder prayers (see Dan. 10:12); he causes sickness and diseases (see Acts 10:38); he deceives people through false prophecies, doctrines and ministers (see 2 Thess. 2:9-10); he discourages, fouls up circumstances, and stirs strife. When we see these things invading our personal world, we know we are engaged in war with a real devil whose only malicious intention is our destruction.

Soldiers Are Armed

The unarmed soldier is useless for battle. The soldiers we want are armed and dangerous. They have weapons. And they know how to use them.

In our organization, we employ over three hundred people between our church and our school. In addition, we have hundreds of pastors and workers all around the world. Before we place someone in a significant leadership role, I want to know what fights they've been in and whether they won, especially a fight involving an offense within the organization. When someone has overcome their offense and in the process is able to defend the place from where the hurt came, then we have a soldier we can trust.

Though we walk in the flesh, we do not war according to the flesh. For the weapons of our warfare are not carnal but mighty in God for pulling down strongholds.

2 Timothy 2:4

4

IMPERATIVE SUCCESS

Successful people hold influence, while those who fail don't. Generally speaking, leadership is gained and kept because of success. Failure quickly erodes whatever respect a leader once commanded.

History shouts that people rally to make him their leader who defeats their enemy; defeated leaders forfeit authority. The wisdom of the wealthy is respected; the wisdom of the poor is unheeded. Those winning against severe competition will lead; the beaten becomes the follower. Problem solvers are given leadership. Innovators bringing prosperity will gain influence; those leaders bringing poverty forfeit respect and therefore influence. A wise but poor or unsuccessful or defeated person won't be accepted as a leader. Success is not an option—it is imperative.

> *Wisdom is better than strength. Nevertheless the poor man's wisdom is despised, and his words are not heard.*
>
> Ecclesiastes 9:16

Successful people learn from other successful people. None of us are successful on our own. None of us with a brain are going to surrender the direction of our lives to people failing in areas in which we are aiming to succeed. The conclusion is that people need to be successful to lead. Leadership does not automatically guarantee success. However, success will give you influence. We must change areas where we fail. Our capacity to change depends on how desperate we are to escape failure. Our success then influences others to be successful in life. So let's get successful—it's not that elusive.

Seven Secrets to Success

1. Identify a need you can meet, then meet it.

Everyone in this world has a need of some sort. Every one of us also has a solution for certain needs. People in hospitals need a visit. Elderly people need someone to read to them. Someone needs help with their grocery shopping or with mowing the lawn. A young guy in our church wanted to make extra cash after school. He decided to offer a free one-time lawn mowing service to some local business parks. They liked what he did so much they gave him the contract. When he left school, he sold the business for $60,000!

2. Identify the hurt you can heal, then heal it.

Everyone gets wounded at some time. All of us have something that brings healing. We don't have to be doctors to heal. A smile, a soothing conversation, or laughter can all bring healing. Kind words to people under pressure. Words of mercy to the guilty. For every person in prison, there most often is a grieving mother at home. There is always something we can do to bring healing to broken people. One of the deepest bonds we can ever make is through bringing healing to a wound in a person's life. Success is not about what I can achieve for me; it's about how adept I am at improving others' lives.

There are thousands of people who have been told by experts that their case is hopeless. And yet it isn't hard to find biographies of people who have ignored the critics, beaten the odds, overcome the diagnoses, and lived brilliant lives. This is where the deepest wound is. When people lose faith, they lose hope and the chance to overcome. All of us can give faith to people. We can believe in them when they can't believe themselves. Whoever believes in others will be given leadership by those same people. We are happy to follow a person who believes in us. Instinctively, we know we will rise higher under them than under some negative sourpuss.

3. **Identify the opportunities you can take advantage of, and take advantage to the max.**

For a farmer, the seasons are his opportunities. He needs to plough in winter, sow in spring, reap in summer, and sell in autumn. If he doesn't, he'll never be a successful farmer. For a pastor, it is about recognizing what age group and what culture he is able to reach and pitching his services to those people.

It is Sir Bruce Small recognizing the potential of a swamp on the east coast of Australia and believing it can become a paradise, a Surfers Paradise. He approached over 90 banks before one finally agreed to fund his dream. Today, that part of the east coast of Australia has spawned a thousand and one different developments, businesses, and communities. It has been copied again and again along the same coast.

Opportunity is Colonel Sanders at the age of sixty-five believing that his mother's fried chicken recipe could be successful as a restaurant meal. After receiving his first retirement check, he wondered if this is all life now amounts to—rocking in his chair on the front porch, waiting for the monthly social security check. He made a list of all the positive things in his life. One of these was his mother's fried chicken. He asked a local restaurant if he could add it to their menu, cook it himself, and see what the response was. His dish soon became the favorite. The rest is history.

When Fred Smith saw an opportunity for overnight delivery of anything anywhere in the USA, and ultrafast delivery anywhere in the world, FedEx was born.

American Express saw the opportunity for delivering checks across the country and cashing them, thus replacing money orders. Soon they saw more opportunities with cards replacing cash. Then they saw that people need quick, easy cash when they travel.

Michael Dell sees the opportunity for inexpensive computers and Dell computers is born.

Howard Schultz smells the opportunity for great coffee in America and Starbucks spreads around the world.

Opportunities are everywhere. If we're awake and searching, we will find them. We fail to see opportunities because of a negative mind-set. A shoe salesman was sent from New York to Africa in the early 1900s. After his first day on the job, he sent an urgent telegram back to head office, saying, "Send me a return ticket immediately. Nobody here wears shoes!" The company sent the ticket and he returned to America. But the shoe company tried again sending a different salesman. When he arrived, he also sent a telegram back: "Send all the shoes you've got. Nobody here wears shoes!" Opportunities lie in the eye of the beholder.

Opportunities need discernment too though. Not everything that glitters is gold. Anything posing as an opportunity generally isn't. Most opportunities come unlabelled. "Get rich quick" schemes, "not to be missed," "never to be repeated"—such so-called opportunities are designed to separate the naive and their money. False opportunities waste so much time and destiny. They derail you from your purpose in life.

The matter of opportunity is too important simply to leave it here. Let's go deeper. Let's grasp how we can maximize our opportunities. The apostle Paul recognized immense opportunity in Ephesus, even though at the same time, he was also faced with immense obstacles.

*A **great** and **effective** door has **opened** to me, and there are many adversaries.*

1 Corinthians 16:9

You've got to love Paul referring to the adversaries with an "and" not a "but"! The spirit of "and" rather than the spirit of "but" is basic to taking advantage of any opportunity. Whatever you're facing right now, put "and" after your description of it and see what you come up with, rather than going with the way too easy "but."

Here are eight principles for maximizing opportunities:

i. *Having momentum*

"...Paul...came to Ephesus." (Acts 19:1).

Paul was on the move and arrived in Ephesus. Under the Romans, Ephesus had thrived. She reached the pinnacle of her greatness during the first and second centuries of the Christian era. At the time of Paul, Ephesus was probably the fourth largest city in the world with a population estimated at 250,000. During the reign of the emperor Hadrian, Ephesus was designated the capital of the Roman province of Asia. With the apostle came a massive revival. Paul decided to maximize the possibilities.

This was Paul's third and final missionary journey, yet he spent nearly three years in this city teaching and preaching in the local synagogue and in the hired hall of an educator called Tyrannus. The power of his preaching ("...*all who dwelt in Asia heard the word of the Lord Jesus...*"[Acts 19:10]) also triggered a riot headed by a group of silversmiths who feared that sales of their miniature replicas of the local goddess, Diana, would suffer (Acts 19:24-41).

People in motion uncover opportunities a thousand times more often than those who are not moving. Sitting around waiting for the big break does not open doors. Momentum positions us for opportunities when they come. Momentum keeps us in place on the field wherever the ball is in play. Momentum is being fit enough to keep up with the play. It is training so that when the ball is passed to you, it's automatic—you catch, you run, you score! The unfit, unmoving, and untrained drop the ball, stumble, and lose. When the ball is passed to the person who is not in position, they don't get it. Someone else does—the guy keeping up with the play.

Be at the meeting. Be up with the latest information. Be in the conference. Phone them. Write a letter. Stay longer. Start earlier. Be helpful in areas you're not paid for. Give gifts. Meet people. Ask to be introduced. Invite someone for dinner. Whatever your game is, there are a thousand opportunities right now waiting to be seized.

The ants are a people not strong, Yet they prepare their food in the summer.

Proverbs 30:25

Even ants are smarter than most people, simply because they take advantage of the season when it's upon them. This is why our Ministry Training College and School of Creative Arts are so powerful. They equip hundreds of young men and women for the future. These people are ready for their opportunities. When someone is looking for a leader, they contact us. When dancers are needed, we get a call.

Peter, James, and John were not just there physically with Jesus climbing the Mount of Transfiguration; they were there spiritually. (Mark 9:2.) Their faith was there. Thomas was not invited up the mountain. Doubt dislocated him from the action. Unbelief positioned him off the field. Questions distanced him from the power of God.

Faith doesn't just believe. It acts. It does things. Faith is always taking steps, making moves, leaping ahead. Faith is not passive. Faith is momentum. Do something! It's the movers who get guidance. We use the steering wheel when the car is moving.

ii. Searching for opportunities

...And finding some disciples...

Acts 19:1

Ask, and it will be given to you; seek, and you will find; knock, and it will be opened to you. For everyone who asks receives, and he who seeks finds, and to him who knocks it will be opened.

Matthew 7:7,8

Paul found some disciples because he went looking for them. We find what we are looking for. Seekers find.

You will receive—if you keep asking!

You will find what you're looking for—if you keep looking!

The door will open—if you keep knocking!

On June 6, 1981, Doug Whitt and his bride, Sylvia, were escorted to their hotel's fancy bridal suite in the small hours of the morning. In the suite they saw a sofa, chairs, and a table, but where was the bed? Then they discovered the sofa was a hide-a-bed, with a lumpy mattress and sagging springs. They spent a fitful night and woke up in the morning with sore backs. The new husband went to the hotel desk and gave the management a tongue-lashing. "Did you open the door in the room?" asked the desk clerk. Doug went back to the room. He opened a door that they had thought was a closet. There, complete with fruit baskets and chocolates, was the beautiful honeymoon bedroom![1]

People often give up way too soon in their search. Fears can paralyze action if we let them. Even initial defeat is no reason to give up. Even though some of the people I mentioned before are enormously successful, things didn't just drop out of the sky for them. Sir Bruce Small approached 95 banks before he got the loan to turn his swamp into Surfers Paradise, Australia. Colonel Saunders approached no less than 1,000 banks, attempting to get a loan for his idea of a fried chicken restaurant chain. Walt Disney went bankrupt before getting Disneyland off the ground. Thomas Alva Edison, patriarch of General Electric, is credited with saying "I failed my way to success," time after time repeating thousands of experiments in attempts to illuminate the light bulb.[2]

We are the ones creating our own opportunities more than anyone else. We are also the ones shutting them down.

After the New Coke debacle of 1985, Coca-Cola chairman Roberto Goizueta said, "The moment you let avoiding failure become your motivator, you're down the path of inactivity. You can only stumble if you're moving. If you don't have a few failures, you're not taking enough chances. Nobody can be right all the time, and the big companies didn't become big by playing it safe."[3]

iii. Taking advantage of opportunities

...Did you receive the Holy Spirit when you believed?...

Acts 19:2

Paul asked the disciples he found if they had progressed in their faith. Their reply told him they needed more and so he led them into a further encounter with God. Taking advantage of the opportunity begins by asking questions, seeking more information, knocking on the door. We must ask questions that open up the opportunity even more. A door has no value unless we go through it. "Opportunities multiply as they are seized." (Sun Tzu).

Abraham Lincoln is credited with saying, "Seize the initiative and never relinquish it."[4]When we lose the initiative so that we are only responding to whatever is coming our way, our position is weak. We are on the back foot, defending ourselves. Front-footed living means I take advantage of the situation first. I seize the initiative and don't allow anyone to take it from me.

When something threatening you has a lapse of weakness, this is your moment of opportunity. Lincoln understood this. His lesson is, "Take advantage of confusion, desperation, and urgency to exercise strong leadership."[5]

Backyard politicians, locker-room businessmen, and armchair athletes all see opportunities. But the only ones with a chance are those who actually do something. Andy Stanley, pastor of the fast-growing North Point Community Church in Atlanta, Georgia, says,

"Leaders are not always the first to *see* an opportunity. They are simply the first to *seize* an opportunity."[6]

Blind Bartimaeus, the beggar of Mark 10:47, was one such opportunist. His healing was walking right next to him. Jesus might see him and initiate healing. Or He might not! This man is not going to let the chance of it not happening occur. He cries out for the Healer. Everyone shouts him down. How could Jesus be interested in this grumpy, irreverent, blind beggar? The man's cries bring the Messiah to a standstill. Jesus calls him. Bartimaeus is healed. A blind man received his sight. Why? He refused to let his moment, his opportunity, slip by.

We can create opportunities out of our seeming disadvantages if we are bold enough. John Kanary tells the story of Charlie Boswell, a man who has inspired thousands to rise above circumstances. Charlie was blinded during World War II while rescuing his friend from a tank under fire. He had been a great athlete before his accident, but now blind he decided to try a brand-new sport, a sport he had never imagined playing, even with his eyesight—golf! Through determination and a deep love for the game he went on to become the National Blind Golf Champion. In fact, he won that title 13 times!

One of Charlie's heroes was the great golfer Ben Hogan, so it was truly an honor for Charlie to win the Ben Hogan Award in 1958. Meeting Ben Hogan, Charlie was awestruck and said his one wish was to have a round of golf with the great Ben Hogan. Mr Hogan agreed that playing a round together would be an honor for him as well, as he had heard all about Charlie's accomplishments and admired his skills.

"Would you like to play for money, Mr Hogan?" Charlie blurted out.

"I can't play you for money. It wouldn't be fair!" said Hogan.

"Aw, come on, Mr Hogan. $1,000 per hole?"

"I can't. What would people think of me, taking advantage of you and your circumstance," replied the golfer.

"Chicken, Mr. Hogan?"

"Okay," exclaimed a frustrated Hogan, "but I am going to play my best!"

"I wouldn't expect anything else," said the confident Boswell.

"Okay, you're on, Mr. Boswell. You name the time and the place!" said Hogan.

Very self-assured, Boswell immediately responded, "10 o'clock—tonight!"[7]

iv. Big things start small

Don't scorn small start-ups.

Do not despise these small beginnings....

Zechariah 4:10 NLT

Great churches generally begin from small groups. There's not a church of thousands that we know of today that started from anything more than a small home group, or a family and some friends getting together.

General Electric, one of the world's largest companies today, being worth more than 250 billion dollars, started with Edison's invention of the lightbulb in 1879. The great nation of America sprang out of a handful of pilgrims emigrating from England in 1620 with a dream. The church of Jesus began with twelve uneducated, inexperienced men in the first century A.D. Great trees always begin from tiny seeds.

Bill Hull notes that one of the giant redwood cedars of California is 270 feet high and weighs 6,300 tons, and comes from a seed weighing just three thousandths of an ounce.[8]

Great opportunities come heavily disguised as small doors or big problems in work clothes. Roy Williams relates the story of Thomas Jefferson constructing the Constitution of the United States of America in 1787; only white male landowners were granted the vote. The poor, the Africans, the Asians, the Indians, and women were not considered equals. America was the land of opportunity only for wealthy white males.

The structure of society in the New World was very much as it had been in the Old World until 1886, when the Statue of Liberty arrived as a gift from the French. In all of America, there was no one among the privileged of 1886 who was willing to undertake the raising of a paltry $100,000 to assemble the Statue of Liberty. Today's America was born in 1886. The Statue of Liberty would have remained in crates to this very day had it not been for the efforts of an immigrant from Hungary. In his little paper, the *New York World,* Joe Pulitzer appealed to the little people of the city to undertake the installation of the statue. Shoeshine boys, chimney sweeps, machine operators, and grocery clerks were called upon to come to the rescue. In recognition of their heroism, Pulitzer published the name of every contributor, even little kids who gave a nickel.

One of the contributors was a young Jewish woman named Emma Lazarus, who wrote a poem for an art exhibition to help raise money for the statue's installation. Emma's poem closed with the following lines: "Give me your tired, your poor, your huddled masses yearning to breathe free, the wretched refuse of your teeming shore.

Send these, the homeless, tempest-tost to me. I lift my lamp beside the golden door!" (I'll bet you thought the government wrote that, didn't you?)

In the end, 121,000 people contributed an average of 83 cents each to erect what has become the most American of all symbols. As a result of his efforts to erect the monument, the circulation of Joe's little paper grew to monumental proportions as well, and Joseph Pulitzer went on to impact our nation as few men have ever done.[9]

v. *Working the extra mile*

He went into the synagogue and spoke boldly for three months, reasoning and persuading concerning the things of the kingdom of God.

Acts 19:8

Success has little to do with luck. Most people succeeding in life have discovered the truth of the saying, "The harder I work the luckier I get!" This adage probably originated with Thomas Jefferson, the hard-working third President of the United States (1801–1809). A member of the second Continental Congress, he drafted the Declaration of Independence in 1776. A political philosopher, educator, and architect, Jefferson designed his own estate, Monticello, and buildings for the University of Virginia. You've got to admit, he was qualified to say, "The harder I work, the more luck I seem to have."

The legendary violin craftsman, Antonio Stradivari affirmed, "If my hand slacked, I should rob God."

A former college roommate remembers former General Electric CEO Jack Welch as a fearsome competitor with average skills: "Jack wasn't blessed with a lot of grace or athletic ability. He trounced people by trying harder."[10]

The call of God comes to busy people. Amos, Moses, and David were all shepherding sheep when they received news of God's purpose for their lives. Peter, James, and John were all fishing when Jesus happened by, calling them to an adventure beyond their wildest dreams. The great apostle Paul was called while he was very busy persecuting the church.

Working hard means:

- Doing the most important work first, especially when we're trying to avoid it because it's the more difficult part of the job;
- Selling when it's easier to be talking and planning;
- Cutting costs when it hurts;
- Saying what people don't want to hear but needs to be said;
- Bugging people who are moving too slowly;
- Firing people who are not working out;
- Writing a book when you want to take the day off!

Hard workers find out what needs to be done and just do it.

Among the most tragic verses of Scripture is Jeremiah repeating the cry of lost people reaching the ears of the prophet:

The harvest is past, the summer is ended, and we are not saved!
Jeremiah 8:20

Those called to lead them to salvation had failed to take advantage of their summertime opportunity. Other people's destinies hang on us grasping our opportunities to reach them.

Jesus chided His generation for failing to recognize their day. The book of Hebrews warns us against repeating the mistake of the Israelites who refused to hear the voice of God that was guiding them into their enormous opportunity. Another major dimension of realizing any opportunity is simply to get off our butts and make it happen.

vi. *Paddling your own canoe*

When some were hardened and did not believe, but spoke evil of the Way before the multitude, he departed from them and withdrew the disciples, reasoning daily in the school of Tyrannus.

Acts 19:9

Paul didn't complain about the fact that he remained unsupported, even opposed, by his own countrymen. Neither did he receive support from those whom he could have reasonably expected it. He understood that "if it is to be, it has to be me." He accepted responsibility for his own circumstances. You can't be relying on others to make your world go round for you. There is only one person responsible for that—that would be you. If we kicked the person responsible for most of our troubles, we wouldn't be able to sit down for a month!

Phil Baker comments

"I am not to blame," has grown in popularity, especially in the last 40 years. It has been sustained by the willingness to believe, fuelled by Freudian psychology, and now fanned white hot by the genetic arguments being advanced for every type of human behaviour and misbehaviour. To be consistent then, we should never claim credit for victories won or goals achieved.

The blame mentality, if correct, would declare that nothing good or bad is ever our fault. This type of fatalism does not wash with most people, so we moderate the harsh reality of taking it to its logical conclusion and develop an irrational philosophy of life…. A philosophy that says we are the reason for our failures. Zig Ziglar has pointed out that we have all heard of the self-made success but never the self-made failure.[11]

No one can do your training for you if you're planning on winning an Olympic medal. No one can fight your wars for you if you're planning on victory. As Mark Twain said, "Don't go around saying the world owes you a living; the world owes you nothing; it was here first."[12]

Those who maximize their opportunities are the people who accept that it's their personal responsibility to do just that. When we search for excuses to explain why we failed, we need to "slap the whiner within." We are better served by discovering our part in the failure. "What did I do wrong?" Then we can learn. We can correct ourselves. The mistakes of our past don't have to shape our future. Anyone can have a fresh start. We don't have to repeat our mistakes. We move from the remorse of poor decisions, learn from failure, gain wisdom we didn't have before, and work with fresh enthusiasm to make the rest of our life a dream coming true.

Zig Ziglar, quoted in Bob Harrison's book, *Power Points for Success*, makes the following point: "Regardless of your past, tomorrow is a clean slate. If you do the things you ought to do when you ought to do them, the day will come when you can do the things you want to do when you want to do them."[13]

vii. *Going all the way*

This continued for two years, so that all who dwelt in Asia heard the word of the Lord Jesus, both Jews and Greeks.

Acts 19:10

Paul continued to preach in Ephesus not just for one week, two weeks, one month, or six months, but for two years. He continued until he had exhausted the opportunity of this great and effectual door. He kept going until he was convinced that all of Asia had heard his message.

One of the worst regrets in life is recognizing an opportunity after the fact, knowing that if we had applied ourselves more aggressively we could have taken full advantage of it. The only way to take full advantage of an opportunity is to be fully committed to it.

"The loss of focus on four or five shots a round makes the difference between great golf and mediocre golf."[14]

In an article for the Christian Heritage Center website, Howard Culbertson writes about an incredible opportunity the church fumbled.[15] A brief window of opportunity opened for the gospel in the Mongolian empire of ancient China. Christianity had been introduced to the Mongols as early as the 8th century by Nestorian Christian missionaries from Persia. However, it was in the 13th century reign of Genghis Khan that there was significant growth of Christianity in Mongolia.

Genghis Khan was married to a Christian woman. One of the Khan's daughters-in-law, Sorkaktani, was a Nestorian Christian who became the mother of three great emperors, including Kublai Khan. A dozen Dominican and Franciscan missionaries were working in Mongolia at that time.

When the opportunity came to join a diplomatic mission to the court of the Mongol emperor Kublai Khan, who ruled China from present-day Beijing, Nicolo Polo, an Italian merchant, seized it. Khan was courteous and friendly toward the visitors and very curious about the western world. He was particularly interested in Christianity and sent the Polos back to Europe as his personal ambassadors. Along with messages of peace, the Khan asked the Pope to send 100 scholars to teach his people about Christianity and western science. After a three-year return trip, the men arrived in Europe only to find Pope Clement IV had died. Immediate return to China was impossible because the family had to await a papal election, an event that took three years. When Pope Gregory X was finally elected, he did send two priests (not 100) and the party set out on the 5,000-mile journey, taking three and a half years.

The history of Christianity among the Mongols is a history of "what ifs." We don't know for sure what would have happened if some things had gone differently. However, there does seem to have been a window of opportunity for Christianity in the Mongol empire that Christians failed to fully exploit.

Joash, the king of Israel from 835-796 B.C., was desperate for guidance. However, the prophet Elisha, who had always provided this, was deathly ill. Joash visited the prophet, asking how he was to defeat the Syrians. The prophet told him to open the east window and then to shoot arrows through it. The king shot three times then stopped. The dying prophet rebuked him for not shooting as many arrows as he could, emptying the quiver. The message is clear. The window of opportunity is realized only as we give it everything we've got. The prophet told the king even though he would enjoy initial victory, this wouldn't last because his halfheartedness would result only in ultimate defeat (see 2 Kings 13:14-19).

One of the most disastrous missed opportunities relates to Mahatma Gandhi, one of the greatest leaders of modern history. A Hindu, Gandhi nevertheless admired Jesus, often quoting from the

Sermon on the Mount. When the missionary E. Stanley Jones met with Gandhi, he asked him, "Mr Gandhi, though you quote the words of Christ often, why is that you appear to so adamantly reject becoming his follower?" Gandhi replied, "Oh, I don't reject your Christ. I love your Christ. It's just that so many of you Christians are so unlike your Christ."

Apparently Gandhi's rejection of Christianity grew out of an incident that had happened when he was a young man practicing law in South Africa. He had become attracted to the Christian faith, had studied the Bible and the teachings of Jesus, and was seriously exploring becoming a Christian. And so he decided to attend a church service. As he went up the steps of the large church where he intended to go, a white South African elder of the church barred his way at the door. "Where do you think you're going, kaffir?" the man asked Gandhi in a belligerent tone of voice. Gandhi replied, "I'd like to attend worship here." The church elder snarled at him, "There's no room for kaffirs in this church. Get out of here or I'll have my assistants throw you down the steps." From that moment, Gandhi decided to adopt what good he found in Christianity but would never again consider becoming a Christian if it meant being part of the church.[16]

We have to learn from these enormous mistakes and remove prejudices and every other obstacle to our God-given opportunities.

Walt Disney needed $800 to start his company. His brother Roy lent him $300. Walt insisted that he become a partner and Roy accepted. Walt's Uncle Robert lent him the other $500 and refused the partnership deal. Roy became a billionaire and one of the wealthiest men in Hollywood, owning half of Disney. Uncle Robert got his $500 back with interest. Bad decision, Uncle Robert!

viii. *Overcoming the obstacles*

Obstacles are the prelude to opportunities. Most opportunities come wrapped in a black box labeled "problem." We can see the opportunity but why are there so many obstacles? These will actually help rather than hinder us. The problem summons strength we never knew we had and lifts us to new levels of commitment we would never have given without the impossible situation. A common enemy galvanises a team. It's not the size of the dog in the fight. It's the size of the fight in the dog. The fight draws out of us far more than we think we have. The desperation aroused in overcoming life-threatening moments surfaces courage and strength that remain undiscovered in comfort. We seek comfort. God seeks our attention. We seek ease. Our dream seeks fulfilment.

Goliath was a big problem. He threatened Israel's entire future. Defeating just one Jewish champion would doom the entire Hebrew nation to servitude under the Philistines. But maybe Goliath was also an opportunity. If he were defeated, Israel would rule the Philistines. Fear is parceled with opportunity—great fear, great opportunity. David didn't start that day seeking to take advantage of an opportunity. He was simply doing what needed to be done—taking fresh supplies to his warrior brothers. But when he heard the roar of Goliath, it was he who rose to the challenge.

Courage maximizes possibilities. Joyce Meyer describes courage as "doing it afraid." Andy Stanley observes, "As I listen to leaders tell their stories, I hear very little about strategic planning and goal setting. I hear a lot about identifying and acting on opportunities. Leaders see and seize opportunity."[17]

Whenever there's opportunity there's opposition. There's always a reason not to do something. Inaction is never difficult to justify. Excuses often parade as explanations. However, your success is discovered in the journey of overcoming the roadblocks opposing your progress.

King Solomon is considered to have been the wisest man in history. One of his brilliant proverbs, found in Ecclesiastes 11:4—*"He who observes the wind will not sow, And he who regards the clouds will not reap,"*—is paraphrased by Kenneth Taylor in *The Living Bible* as follows: *"If you wait for perfect conditions, you will never get anything done."* Written almost 3,000 years ago, this insight confirms that the human predilection to justify inaction is perennial. We all want to avoid the difficult, even though it is there that we find success.

Solomon, unaffected by today's thinking that classifies such behaviour as a disorder, or the result of a damaged early life, or a genetic malfunction, simply calls it what it is—laziness. In Proverbs 22:13 NLT, "The lazy person is full of excuses. 'I can't go to work!' he says. 'If I go outside I might meet a lion in the street and be killed!'" Solomon reveals the level of stupidity we're prepared to go to in order to justify inaction. The lazy invent problems, convincing themselves why they should not venture into the marketplace. All they manage to achieve, however, is to reveal how consumed they are with self-interest, not to mention how spineless they are as well. If there is a lion in the streets, what an opportunity to face, fight, and defeat the beast and deliver the town from the danger! Solomon's perception is that this condition is not a disorder; it is simply a lazy person finding a way to get out of doing something. If we are lazy (and we all are in some area), then we need to take the first step on the pathway to courage and admit it, which is not easy. Then we simply have to put our teeth together and do whatever indolence has prevented.

It all depends on whether we have a "but" mind-set or an "and" mind-set. Alexander Graham Bell, inventor of the telephone, said, "When one door closes another door opens; but we often look so long and so regretfully upon the closed door that we do not see the ones which open for us.[18]

Under Moses, the newly freed Hebrews were dragged by their heels to the beautiful Promised Land. Each step forward uncovered fresh difficulties. Everyone imagined Moses would have them liberated after his first summit with Pharaoh. Instead the outcome of the summit was that life for the Hebrews became twice the hell it had been before. Pharaoh was enraged that they would even imagine leaving Egypt. He demanded twice as many bricks from them with half the resources. Taskmasters were commanded to whip them into achieving their new impossible quotas. The Hebrews lived in agony. They lost faith in the vision and the visionary. With hindsight, however, we see God allowing the problem to enlarge. Why? So that His power would be seen on a grander scale.

When we're drowning in a problem and our emotions are chafed in defeat, this perspective may as well be on Mars. We don't get it. Eventually, however, after a multitude of miraculous judgments on Egypt, the Hebrew slaves are emancipated. They march victoriously into the desert just beyond the city. Soon though, with parched mouths they are searching for water. When they find some, it turns out to be poisoned. Bitterly complaining, they receive a miracle from God. The waters are healed when Moses throws a branch into the pool. Then they hunger for meat. They complain. Quail falls from the sky, till they are knee deep in birds. Still they fail to learn, lurching from one problem to the next, from one complaint to the next, from one miracle to the next, never getting the fact that every impossibility is a catalyst for a miraculous opportunity. Rather than speaking faith when they meet with difficulties, they complain. Finally arriving at their Promised Land, they discover it is infested with giants. Even after the litany of lessons of the journey thus far, they still prefer complaining to believing. They demand that they turn back without even trying to possess the Promised Land across the river Jordan. God is finally too upset with this crowd to allow them access to their beautiful land. He gives them over to their own prediction—"We are doomed to wander the desert and die" (Num. 14:2)—rather than try to drag them forward one more time. Everyone aged over twenty dies over the next forty years (averaging 300 funerals each day!) as they wander around the desert aimlessly.

The message is fearful. We cannot afford to let our unbelief, fears, laziness, or unwillingness prevent us from appropriating our promised destiny. We have only one life. We can't let it slip through our fingers simply because we wouldn't at least have a go at it.

> ...the land...truly flows with milk and honey, and this is its fruit. Nevertheless the people who dwell in the land are strong...Then Caleb quieted the people before Moses, and said, "Let us go up at once and take possession, for we are well able to overcome it." But the men who had gone up with him said, "We are not able to go up against the people, for they are stronger than we." And they gave the children of Israel a bad report of the land which they had spied out, saying, "The land through which we have gone as spies is a land that devours its inhabitants, and all the people whom we saw in it are men of great stature. There we saw the giants...and we were like grasshoppers in our own sight, and so we were in their sight."

So all the congregation lifted up their voices and cried, and the people wept that night. And all the children of Israel complained against Moses and Aaron, and the whole congregation said to them, "If only we had died in the land of Egypt! Or if only we had died in this wilderness! Why has the Lord brought us to this land to fall by the sword, that our wives and children should become victims? Would it not be better for us to return to Egypt?" So they said to one another, "Let us select a leader and return to Egypt."

Numbers 13:27-28,30-33; 14:1-4

4. Be committed to excellence.

Do the job well—better than others. It's amazing how little it takes to do something better, to excel. It's a tradesman replying to a request within 24 hours, doing the job swiftly, and cleaning up after himself. This generates referrals, repeat business, and higher-priced jobs. He becomes successful. It's arriving at your new job half an hour earlier and leaving half an hour later. Excellence is an attitude. It's pride in what you do so you look at your output and feel great that you have done the best you can.

Living as unto God means we exert ourselves to be the best, do the best, and achieve the best, simply because it's for Him. We're carrying His reputation in our hands!

5. Be successful.

Arrange success. If you are successful, you will be more successful. This means if I am successful in doing a great job, I will become successful in that line of work. Success is not just something you become. Success is something we are right now. There are very simple reasons people make themselves successful or not.

If you're starting a church, you make it very hard for yourself if you hire a hall for 500 when you have only 20 people. Much better to hire a small restaurant and pack people in. Don't just assume people will turn up. Make sure they do—call them! "Ring and bring"—all the time. Visit groups and gatherings of all the kinds of people whom you could relate to well and invite them along. Think of all the things that might cause them to think they would like to come back. Never build for this week. Always build for next week. Talk about the vision, what you see the future holding. Make it so attractive that they will invite their family and friends next week. Then explain that you've run out of room and hire a bigger restaurant. It's vital to dream, but we shouldn't build on our dreams. Build on need. One step at a time as the need grows will get you where you want to go.

6. Communicate your story

"Churchill mobilized the English language and sent it into battle."[19] Success breeds success. Whatever I want to achieve, I simply focus everyone on that point by using every means I have. The effective leader points people in the direction they are meant to be going. Without direction people wander aimlessly. This is the point of leadership. We are meant to take people somewhere.

Often, it will be somewhere they don't want to go, so the skill that convinces followers of the journey comes through communicating the vision, the goals, and the strategy to get there. If I am raising money for a building project, I preach on it. I also ask people to tell their stories of the benefits they have received through giving. We create up-market brochures and magazines that send the signal that we are serious about raising serious amounts of money. We regularly reinforce the message to our leaders. Our people must be refocused regularly. Everyone gets distracted. When we are distracted, our resources, energy, time, relationships, and money go to the distraction.

Leaders' constant tasks are continually to bring our primary purpose to the forefront. Leaders' pride can prevent us from repeating ourselves, casting the vision again and again. Yet this is the fuel of the organization. People are fired up by the vision. It reminds them why they are doing what they do, why they are going the extra mile, why they are making the sacrifices.

Never be afraid to shout from the rooftops the good news of what you're doing. Jesus tells us to let our good works shine before others so they will glorify God (see Matt. 5:16). Some think we should never communicate good achievements, believing it is somehow wrong. It's wrong only when we're feeding our ego and elevating ourselves over others. Jesus also warns against that (see Matt. 6:1). However when our purpose is to direct people's attention toward achievements that glorify God, then we should publish with all our might far and wide. When we achieve our goals, we need to communicate the facts to the entire marketplace. We also need to celebrate the success with everybody who helped on the journey. It's also vital to keep your clients' confidence in what you do. This is the bottom line. This confidence flows from your staff and others whom you don't perceive as clients but who endorse what you do. Tell your accountant, your bank manager, your lawyer all the good things that are happening for you. Marketing isn't just something that you get someone else to do. It begins with you. If you're sold on what you're doing, thousands of others will be too. No amount of marketing genius can atone for zero enthusiasm. And no amount of publicity will redeem a downward-trend line on your graphs unless you, the leader, are personally passionate and excited about all you're doing. That's what initiates the turnaround. Love what you do and do what you love.

7. Be organized.

There's often very little between first and second place, between those who grow and those who don't, those who succeed and those who fail. Being organized just one inch more than the other guy can get you across the line first. A person phoned two colleges where she was considering studying. One of the colleges was ours. We have a 24-hour turnaround policy on any requests. This means we return the letter, e-mail, phone call, text message, whatever, within 24 hours. She received a return phone call within a day and a prospectus and application form in a few more days. The other college sent her their forms eighteen months later! She had already completed a year of study with us before the other college's forms arrived!

People will judge us to be uncaring and lacking integrity when we're unorganized. Their criticism will not be "they're unorganized"; it will be "they don't care" or, if you're late with money, "they're not reliable." Leading an organization is exactly that—overseeing a particular set of systems, priorities, times, positions, and everything else that relates to being organized.

Being organized equips me to respond to people:

- Quickly

- Effectively

- Exceeding their expectations

- Taking them further than they anticipated

- Systematically without losing the personal touch

Success is not an elusive mystery reserved for those who are lucky. A survey conducted among prison inmates revealed that most of them believe that successful people have either done wrong but not been caught or are just lucky. The answers obtained from the same survey conducted among successful people were that success comes from hard work, being responsible, and definitely not trusting in luck. Hmmm…which answers to heed?

According to urban legend, Bill Gates, the wealthiest man in the world today with an estimated worth of $100 billion and leader of Microsoft Corporation, one of the most successful companies of all time, once offered these eleven rules for the would-be wealthy:[20]

Rule 1: Life is not fair—get used to it.

Rule 2: The world won't care about your self-esteem. The world will expect you to accomplish something *before* you feel good about yourself.

Rule 3: You will *not*make $40,000 a year straight out of high school. You won't be a vice president with a car phone until you earn both.

Rule 4: If you think your teacher is tough, wait till you get a boss. He doesn't have tenure.

Rule 5: Flipping burgers is not beneath your dignity. Your grandparents had a different word for burger flipping—they called it opportunity.

Rule 6: If you mess up, it's not your parents' fault, so don't whine about your mistakes; learn from them.

Rule 7: Before you were born, your parents weren't as boring as they are now. They got that way from paying your bills, cleaning your clothes, and listening to you talk about how cool you are. So before you save the rain forest from the parasites of your parents' generation, try delousing the closet in your own room.

Rule 8: Your school may have done away with winners and losers, but life has not. In some schools they have abolished failing grades, and they'll give you as many times as you want to get the right answer. This doesn't bear the slightest resemblance to *anything* in real life.

Rule 9: Life is not divided into semesters. You don't get summers off and very few employers are interested in helping you find yourself. Do that on your own time.

Rule 10: Television is *not* real life. In real life, people actually have to leave the coffee shop and go to work.

Rule 11: Be nice to nerds. Chances are you'll end up working for one.

Success is not that hard either. It's only hard if we're not prepared to work, get smart, and do things we don't want to do. First, understand that prosperity and success are the will of God:

> *Beloved, I pray that you may prosper [succeed] in all things and be in health, just as your soul prospers.*
>
> 3 John 2

We also need to understand, however, that this prosperity in its best meaning is prospering from the inside out ("as your soul prospers"). This means success in our soul is foundational to real success in life.

Great attitudes shape the foundation of a successful soul. Here are some Dennis Waitley' truisms that help define that attitude:[21]

- Losers let it happen; winners make it happen.

- Losers step on flowers in search of weeds; winners pull up weeds while enjoying the fragrance of the flowers.

- Losers always have an excuse; winners always have an idea.

- Losers identify with problems; winners identify with solutions.

- Losers say "It's not my fault"; winners say "Let me help you."

- Losers see a problem for every answer; winners see an answer for every problem.

- Losers are down on life and high on drugs; winners are down on drugs and high on life.

- Losers fix the blame; winners fix the situation.

- Losers see the thunderstorms and icy streets; winners see rainbows and ice skates.

- Losers say, "Why don't they do something?"; winners say "Here's something I'm going to do."

- Losers are failure conscious; winners are success conscious.

- Losers do it to others and split; winners do it for others.

- Losers say, "It might be possible, but it's too difficult"; winners say "It might be difficult, but it's always possible."

Betty Anderson Stanley (1904) characterises success as follows:

He has achieved success who has lived well, laughed often and loved much; who has enjoyed the trust of pure women, the respect of intelligent men and the love of little children; who has filled his niche and accomplished his task; who has left the world better than he found it, whether by an improved poppy, a perfect poem, or a rescued soul; who has never lacked appreciation of Earth's beauty or failed to express it; who has always looked for the best in others and given them the best he had; whose life was an inspiration; whose memory a benediction.[22]

Soul success is self-respect born of an honorable life. This means my character is straight, my integrity intact, and my conscience clear. My words match my actions and my intentions are unselfish. I am motivated by a love for people and God. I am prepared to keep promises even when it disadvantages me.

It is better to possess great character than great wealth. Ecclesiastes 7:1 observes that it is better to own a good reputation than expensive oils. It is better if people know you as honest rather than rich but dishonest. Success is soon wrecked on weak character.

Elvis Presley, one of the great heroes of rock and roll, gained the world but died face down, smothered by his shag-pile carpet at the age of 42. Grossly overweight at the time of his death, a postmortem examination and numerous testimonies from acquaintances revealed a tragic addiction to diet pills, sleeping pills, and medications of all descriptions.

Enduring prosperity is founded on character. Character is founded on discipline. Those disciplines maintaining the ways of God invite blessing. Doing things that please God brings prosperity. Things that displease God invite disaster.

He who covers his sins will not prosper, but whoever confesses and forsakes them will have mercy.

Proverbs 28:13

Here are some rudimentary rules for winning in our organizations:

Rule 1: Commitment

Commit to what you do. Don't be wanting to do something else. Give yourself 100 percent to what you do, not because you have to, but because you love what you do. If we love what we do, everybody around us will catch the passion.

Rule 2: Share rewards

Treat the people on your team as partners in a common purpose. If your team members feel included and respected, they will give 100 percent and more to your vision. If they feel like just another cog in the machine, they'll behave as such. I ask people for their input on everything except the overarching vision. I could care less how we get there. If the leader is precious about methods, they lose people. If people feel they have a say in the process and their methods are implemented, even though it might not be the way you would have done it, the win far outweighs the sacrifice.

When the people on your team are listened to, they bring their hearts to the table. When they are bound and gagged and simply told to do as you tell them, their hearts stay at home with their personal worlds. They arrive on time, leave on time, and claim all that is due them, and you have a worker but not a team player. A person whose heart is in the work arrives early, works harder and longer than they need to, makes sacrifices when needed, and loves seeing their part in the process help to achieve the finished product. The smart leader will then give the team player all the credit for his or her part. This kind of team will perform beyond your wildest expectations.

Rule 3: Motivation

Motivate your team. Recognition beats money and ownership for motivation. Achieving high goals and completing projects everyone is proud of puts fuel in everybody's tank. Be enormously and unexpectedly generous and people will return in like manner.

Rule 4: Communication

The more we know, the more confident we are. Why? Because we have "light," knowledge. The more we understand, the more we "get" why we're doing what we're doing. We see the big picture. When people carry the vision as a cause, they tap into hidden power and determination. Information is always power. Information empowers the team.

Rule 5: Appreciation

Knowing the boss noticed and receiving an expression of thanks is something not a lot of people experience. Flattery is compliments without a heart of gratitude and it is easily detected. Encouragement always includes the giver's thankful heart. Nothing can substitute for well-chosen, well-timed, sincere words of praise. They're free, yet they're worth a fortune.

Rule 6: Celebration

Take time out to celebrate victories. Make your failures humorous. Bishop Joseph Garlington, Senior Pastor of Covenant Church of Pittsburgh, says, "If it's funny later, it's funny now." Never take yourself too seriously. If you're free, everyone else will be too.

Rule 7: Listen

Everyone on your team has something worthwhile to say (otherwise, why are they there?). Arrange ways to get people talking. It's vital to know why people are buying, selling, coming, going, joining, leaving. Your frontline team people are the ones who know what's really going on out there. Ask them questions for answers you may not like hearing but need to hear.

Rule 8: The extra mile

Exceed everyone's expectations. People will talk. One way or another they will talk. If you deliver below expectations, the news will spread even quicker. Give people what they thought they asked for, but give something extra as well. When people know you appreciated their coming to your church because you gave them more than they expected, they'll return—with friends. You have to be different to make a difference.

Rule 9: Efficiency

Reigning in the overheads of a growing organization is a constant exercise calling for vigilance and courage. Saying "no" to people when they want the new thing, can't do without this gadget, want to hire new staff, or need new equipment takes great wisdom to keep their hearts and souls alive to the vision when you're not letting expenses run you out of business. Control your expenses. Even the most brilliant organizations can fail if they're running inefficiently.

Rule 10: Uniqueness

Understand your unique distinctions and run with them. Know what you love and are enthusiastic about. Don't get caught up in good ideas—there are thousands of those. Follow the "God" ideas, the ideas that add up to a divine revelation in every way. This might mean ignoring what everyone else says can and can't be done. Spend time meditating about this. Get it right. Write it down. What are you really, really good at? What do you love doing? What works?

5

STRONG AS AN OX

Where no oxen are, the trough is clean; but much increase comes by the strength of an ox.

Proverbs 14:4

The strong can do what the weak cannot. The strong successfully resist what the weak don't. Strength doesn't give up. Strength continues when others wilt. Strength carries the heavy loads. Strength breaks through, creating momentum. Strength clears the way. Strength supports the weak. Strength resists relentless thoughts, lifts up heavy emotions, and carries the burden of care without caving in. The weak leader crumbles under anxiety, drops the ball when it gets too heavy, and falls before powerful opposing forces.

Strength calls people to work, offering no reward. Strength calls for sacrifice from those following. Strong leadership holds to a course without deviating under pressure to a weaker option. Strength moves forward despite criticism and opposition. Strength stands alone in an unpopular decision. Strength holds fast to the plan even when it brings pain. Strength keeps standards when friends relax theirs.

When Joshua, the general of Israel's army, succeeds Moses, he is commanded to be strong. Having served Moses for 40 years, he understands what it is to be obedient to leadership. Those qualified to rule have learned to obey. Close to Moses, he accompanied him in his most intimate encounters with God. Now it is his turn for strong leadership based on encounters with God.

The exhortation to Joshua to be bold, strong, unafraid, and not dismayed came from three different sources:

1. God

"Have I not commanded you? Be strong and of good courage; do not be afraid, nor be dismayed…" (Josh. 1:9).

2. Moses

Then Moses called Joshua and said to him in the sight of all Israel, "Be strong and of good courage…" (Deut. 31:7).

3. The congregation

"…Only be strong and of good courage" (Josh. 1:18).

"Be strong" is a command; therefore, we can obey it. Strength is a choice. We can choose to be strong. Even though we're weak, we can choose to be strong. Strength is a choice.

Inner strength is just like physical strength—it increases with exercise. Any weight trainer knows that resistance increases strength. The battles we fight will strengthen us, not weaken us. Opposition's purpose is to make us victorious, not defeated.

Now there was a long war between the house of Saul and the house of David. But David grew stronger and stronger, and the house of Saul grew weaker and weaker.

2 Samuel 3:1

Success grows from building on our strengths. How do we make our life successful? By building on our strengths!

Your revelation is your strength. What is revelation to you? What insights do you have? These are your strengths.

Identify your weaknesses. Write them down. In your weakness you can be strong. Christ's strength is perfected in weakness (see 2 Cor. 12:9). How? It begins with faith. This comes from revelation in the Word of God. We can build ourselves up by speaking the Word of God relevant to ourselves.

Do you find it hard to forgive? Speak the Word on forgiveness: "...*Forgive, and you will be forgiven*" (Luke 6:37). Go ahead—say it!

Do you need to overcome fear? Speak the Scriptures: "...*God has not given us a spirit of fear...*" (2 Tim. 1:7), "*Fear not, for I am with you...*" (Isa. 41:10) says the Lord!

Your mouth is the keyboard and your brain is the computer. You input the Word into the computer—your mind—through your mouth—the keyboard. Keep on doing this and eventually revelation, light, and faith weave their way into who you are. Your character changes.

You plant the seed of the Word. You keep speaking it. It grows a new you. You have a great attitude—thankful, humble, positive, encouraging, generous, merciful, respectful, patient, joyful, peaceful, and thoughtful. You're honest. You build trust. You believe in what you're doing. You're confident and enthusiastic about all you're doing.

You don't imagine success is automatic. You make success. You inject success into your world.

You flow with the vision of your church. That's why blessing rests on you. Build His church and you'll be blessed. Success comes from white-hot enthusiasm for what you do. You eat it, dream it, pray it, breathe it, live it, think it, and prepare it all the time. It burns in you.

You give the vision goals.

You work with lists.

You are organized.

You have a priority list.

You do first things first, then the second things, then the third things.

You love what you're doing. You revel in it! You smile.

You hustle. You get the people you want. You go after what you want.

You work hard at every area.

You talk about everything with your team. You build the team around you. You believe in them. You tell them they can do it.

You recognize their achievements. You honor the leaders.

You glorify the common man. You teach them what the Word says about what they do. You engage them in your world. You share everything from your secrets to your success with them. You reward them.

You take every chance to promote your projects to your people. You network those who can help you. You maintain relationships with anybody and everybody who can help your dream.

Great followers make great leaders. We make our leaders great. The Bible speaks almost exclusively about us submitting ourselves to our leaders rather than leaders assuming leadership over us. It's a mistake to take rule over people that they haven't given us. On the other hand, we set ourselves up for success when we allow ourselves to be guided by someone we respect as our leader. Good followers make leaders even better than they would normally be. Great followers make great leaders.

Rick Warren, pastor of the great Saddleback Community Church in California and author of the hugely successful book, *The Purpose Driven Life* (one of the highest-selling hardbacks in American history), says of his own attitude towards authority, "I learn as much as I can from as many people as I can." He also teaches, "While you cannot grow a church trying to be someone else, you *can* grow a church by using principles someone else discovered and then filtering them through your personality and context."[1]

When our time for leadership arrives, we will reap what we have sown over our years as followers. If we have been easy to lead, that spirit will be passed on to those we lead. They will not be troublesome to lead. If we have been difficult to lead, that same spirit will pervade our own followers. Our degree of authority will ever be equal only to our degree of submission.

All our lives we are making the crucial choice as to whom we give our loyalty. Our strength is found not in our resistance to authority but in yielding to it. The chain of command is the chain of impartation. Strength from above flows to us through a chain. If we step to the side of that chain assuming our own authority, we remove ourselves from receiving strength that was to be ours. Strength shows itself in several ways:

Leading the Strong

"…Much increase comes by the strength of an ox" (Prov. 14:4).

The farmers of Solomon's day relied on oxen for their productivity. Ministers are "oxen" in church life (see 1 Cor. 9:9). If they are strong, they bring increase. The level of increase reflects the strength of the ministers. The team leader must master the ability to harness the strengths of the strong.

Strong people have opinions, definite purpose, ambitions, and goals. They know they can achieve significant results themselves. So why would they remain in your team helping you to achieve yours?

In commercial operations, we can woo high performers with large salaries and generous perks. But in churches or volunteer organizations, different dynamics motivate the strong. First, the strong do not follow the weak. Inevitably, relationships encounter moments of conflict. If we compromise our stand by yielding to the strong, hoping not to lose them, we will lose them. Sometimes we may need to find middle ground, but a wise leader knows how to be strong and stay with his purpose while also keeping the strong on his side. For the strong, respect is inevitable. A contentious person might leave at the point of conflict, but others on the team will square away their shoulders, gaining new pride in their fearless leader.

Great leaders possess the skill of keeping strong players committed to the vision. If there is a test of wills, it may not always be a win-win situation. The strong simply need to fall in line with the direction you have marked out. Strong people don't always immediately agree. However, I've regularly been amazed at the ability of mature people to go away, think it through, and find a way to reach an agreement with their leader. Trying to convince a person they're wrong and you're right immediately after announcing your intentions is expecting too much. Also, we lose respect for the person who too quickly abandons passionately held beliefs.

Here are three more keys to strong leadership:

1. Strong leadership requires something from others.

Strength isn't always looking for consensus before action. Strength requires people to do things. It may even fall in the line of a command. This means I can call on someone to do something for no other reason than that I am their leader. I don't have to pay them money. I don't have to promise any reward. It is simply the ability to require a person to do something.

A leader is a lawgiver. It is required of leaders that they create order. This order exists because there are laws. In society, those who rule are the lawgivers. It might seem incongruous to be simultaneously issuing rules and caring for people. Genuine care provides people with pathways. Leaders lay clear expectations on their people so they understand how to behave. Without order, weak leaders are constantly dealing with chaos. Order created through rule saves the leader immense amounts of unnecessary wasted energy and time. Leadership burnout can be the result of simply not having had the strength to hold people accountable to a set of rules governing their house.

Some leaders in our church have struggled with this at times, with disastrous consequences. People with great ministry skills can be positioned as leaders even though not proven as leaders. Ministry skills do not substitute for leadership skills. Churches grow from a healthy mixture of leadership and ministry. Great leaders don't always possess great ministry and not all great ministries enjoy leadership skills. Those in positions of responsibility above their leadership ability crumble under the ensuing pressures. Understand though that leadership can be learned, and not only learned, but also increased.

One of our leaders once staged a large production in our city. He enlisted various musicians from our congregation. However, he couldn't seem to call on these people to volunteer their time and skills without offering them money. He didn't cast a vision that inspired people to serve without financial reward. I don't believe we should abuse people and their talents—I'm happy to pay for skill. But this leader was supposed to keep to an approved budget. When he exceeded it by about $70,000, I hit the roof! After I had calmed down a little, I warned him that this could not happen again. Unfortunately, it did and I had to let him go.

A big part of leading is sticking to the budget and raising volunteers or only attempting what is within the scope of our resources. When we do what we can do, God will do what we can't. But when we try to do His part, we will find ourselves in trouble.

2. Strong leadership holds people accountable.

People do what is inspected, not what is expected. Strength is not just the capacity to ask people to do things. It's also being able to hold them accountable. Accountability has to be measurable. That means whatever we are requiring needs to have a number attached to it. I have thought, *I'm reasonably good at this,* until I see my friend Pastor Kong Hee, leader of the incredible City Harvest Church in Singapore, in action. He seems to do nothing without attaching numbers. For example, if a man needs to spend more time with his wife, I would just say, "You need to spend more time at home with your wife." Pastor Kong says, "Spend at least three nights at home with your wife each week." Where I might say everybody in the congregation needs to sing and create a great atmosphere of praise, Pastor Kong says a service needs to reach 105 decibels from the floor before it has reached the level of a great atmosphere for God.

This is a great way to lead because you can always measure whether or not you or your people are rising to an expectation. Strength holds people accountable to expectations. But that's what leadership is—setting the goals and holding the team and ourselves accountable to them.

3. Strong leadership is fearless of the opinions of others.

The leader cannot be held to ransom by the people he leads. People respect strength even if they don't totally agree with you. Weakness inspires no trust at all. Followers tire of weak leadership. As we point our team in the direction of the plan God has for us, we are uncaring of negative opinions. Our foundation comes from hearing God, consulting with our team, and gaining confirmation from those we respect.

Leading Under Criticism

Opposition is the natural environment of effective leaders. Resisting extreme reaction to criticism is the key to steadiness at the helm.

One of the most difficult challenges for a leader is to cope with the inevitable criticism that comes from being out in front. In fact, the more successful you become the greater the criticism will be. People clothe jealousy, prejudice, and envy with plausible-sounding criticisms.

Henry Louis Mencken (1880-1956) said "Criticism is prejudice made plausible."[3] In a letter to John Wesley, George Whitefield wrote:

Through good and ill report I still rushed on,
Nor felt the fire of popular applause
Nor feared the torturing flame in such a glorious cause.[4]

Even though Billy Graham enjoys great widespread respect and honor today, there was a day when the newspapers, the radio, and especially local religious hierarchies were totally critical of him. To his credit, he handled these tirades with grace. Criticism hurts, especially when it comes from those we would expect to be supportive of us, those we imagine to hold the same aims.

When our cause is grand enough, this helps to engulf all the wounding that criticism is designed to inflict. Keeping a good attitude, the leader must develop a tough heart. Not a hard heart, just tough. It copes with criticism. It's about having the hide of a rhinoceros and the heart of sheep. The only way to handle the critics is to choose to love them. This is the answer Jesus has for them too: Love your enemies. Pray for them and bless them (Matt. 5:44). This not only defuses the critic, but also locates our attitude in the right climate. Give gifts to the angry critic. Bless them. Remember Christ on the Cross at Calvary forgiving those who put Him there.

Leading the Loyal and the Disloyal

To state the obvious once again, great leadership rises on great character. Most often, however, the "king-maker" is courage. The courageous become leaders—the guy who takes on the giant, who defies the odds, who risks all and wins, who warms the ardor of people. Things like talent, wisdom, success, problem-solving, or charisma can also bring a person to leadership. However, no matter what initially brings us leadership, it is character that maintains it.

Integrity determines whether or not we retain the loyalty and respect of our followers.

A leader generally has a highly choleric personality. According to the DISC personality profiling system, they are a "D" type personality. This type of person gives loyalty but also demands it. When trust is breached, they feel it deeply.

Once I asked Hal Oxley, whom I greatly respect, what his thoughts were on disloyalty. He replied, "Philip, I have been in three vocations—the military, industry, and the ministry. In the military, if a man was disloyal, he was shot! In the world of industry, if a person was found disloyal, they were immediately shown the door. In the ministry I have adopted the same attitude. Disloyalty cannot be tolerated for a minute!"

Loyalty is really seen only when a person is under pressure to be disloyal. The church is like a tent for the presence of God. A tent is secured to the earth by ropes tied to deeply driven stakes. Loyalty is the stake in the ground we rely on for our tent to be secure. God arranges situations that "...*strengthen your stakes*..."(Isa. 54:2). We are meant not simply to be connected but committed.

All of us are destined to be in relationships that are divine connections. These are not simply natural relationships. These are God connections for His purpose. In fact, no purpose God has for us excludes other people. None of us has our entire destiny within ourselves (see Jer. 10:23). My reckoning is that about 90 percent of our destiny lives in those we are connected to. The pieces of our puzzle hide within people around us. The scripture "...*What God has joined together, let not man separate*" (Matt. 19:6) has a wider application than just marriage. Our divine connections are the key to our success. That's why Satan works to destroy these relationships. When we lose connectedness, we lose destiny.

Fellowship is one thing but loyalty is another. I have fellowship with people everywhere, but I am called to be loyal to those people I recognize God connects me with.

A test of loyalty prepares us for the pressures that come on our relationships when we succeed or fail. We are tested when those we are loyal to question our loyalty. We are tested when we feel we have justifiable criticisms of those same people, our leaders.

Disloyalty finds its root in unresolved offenses. Unhealed offenses fester. Unresolved issues breed ill will. Bitterness leaves us vulnerable to dark traces of disloyalty. Harboring offenses nurtures breaches that we eventually justify with an eye-for-an-eye rationale.

We break faithfulness when our perspective is short-term. If we choose immediate personal benefit at the cost of remaining loyal, our decisions will be flawed. If our allegiance is to outcomes rather than people, we inevitably isolate ourselves from those relationships that ultimately build our lives. This is a mistake. Great decisions are birthed from a commitment to integrity rather than results. There is a right and there is a wrong. Sometimes doing right will disadvantage us. This is the price of integrity. The psalmist declares that the person who wishes to ascend the hill of God will swear to his own hurt (Ps. 15:4).

The life of King David's son Absalom is a story of the test of loyalty all of us will face at some time. Absalom's story covers seven chapters of biblical history, from 2 Samuel 13 to chapter 20. It's a story of people forced to choose between loyalties. The quality of their choices reflects the quality of their character.

Absalom's treachery originates with his brother Amnon being "sick with love" for his beautiful sister Tamar. (Maybe we should say he's just sick!) Failing to quash his lust, he enlists his friend Jonadab into arranging for her to come to his bedroom. Amnon rapes her. Immediately after the rape, disgusted with himself and what has happened, and with all traces of affection vaporized, he kicks his sister out. Utterly shamed, she leaves unwanted and disgraced.

Absalom also deeply loves his sister Tamar but as a sister. So much so that he names his own daughter after her (see 2 Sam. 14:27). He is the eldest son of David, and his sense of responsibility runs deep. For whatever reason, King David, Tamar's father, does nothing. Into this vacuum of justice, Absalom schemes to avenge the rape of his sister. He waits two years and then hosts a celebration for all the king's sons at the close of shearing season. It's a ruse that lures Amnon into a death trap. Absalom kills Amnon during the festivities and then flees from Jerusalem to Geshur, banished by his own father.

Failed justice sours Absalom's attitude. No judgment has been handed down against Amnon for the rape, and when the avenger finally metes out justice, instead of being approved he is rejected. He broods in Geshur while David mourns his fugitive son every day. After three years, David asks him to return, but still refuses to see him personally.

After a complex intercession by Joab (David's general), Absalom finally meets with his father, but his estrangement has by now morphed into treason. He positions himself at the gate of the city, the place where the king and other elders and dignitaries meet, where major political and commercial transactions take place, the place where all the influential leaders of the town gather. He begins to woo the people. Absalom has always been very handsome. He is attractive. He knows how to charm. He opines that if he were their leader, then they would have someone to hear their cases properly. He passes judgment on people's lawsuits outside the court, telling them their cases are good and right. He kisses their hands. He creates an aura of importance by surrounding himself with a military escort. He parades as their next leader. *"…So Absalom stole the hearts of the men of Israel"* (2 Sam. 15:6).

When God selects servants, they are resourced, promoted, and endorsed by Him, not themselves. The currently recognized leader endorses the successor, just as John the Baptist did with Jesus, Moses with Joshua, and David with Solomon. People arranging for their own promotion in a kingdom that belongs not to them but to God leads to ruin. Let's discuss this for a moment.

Paul declares that all authority is arranged by God. No one really has authority within himself or herself. All authority comes from God. We have as much authority as He gives us. If we are submitted to God, then His authority flows through us. As we execute His will and not ours, His authority endorses our calling as a leader. Without miraculous signs and wonders, Moses would not have convinced the Hebrews that he was their deliverer. The apostles were authenticated as God's appointed leaders to the early church and to the world at large by the manifestation of signs, wonders, and miracles. Jesus himself appealed to the miracles that accompanied Him as validation that He was sent from God. The conclusion is that we need to accept the influence of those men and women endorsed by signs that accompany their message from God.

Any message from God will see fulfilment in reality, not just in words. The simplest example of this is that if a person is called by God into leadership, then people will gather to that person. Gideon blew a trumpet and all Israel gathered to him (Judges 6:34). History has endured instances of the ambitious and impatient, so badly craving leadership that they have blown their own trumpets to announce their own coronation, isolated from any divine approval.

The kingdom of God is not ours. We are His servants. We are not leaders unless we are His servants. Serving Him, He establishes and authenticates our calling. Most people God calls are reluctant to take on the job. Those of us too eager for the role may have been blinded by the power and privileges of leadership but we've avoided looking at the price tag.

When God does call us to leadership, the timing for release is critical. The vision comes early in our life, but the fulfillment of that call will be years or even decades later. Joseph saw his future when just seventeen, and yet he had to journey through certain preparations readying him for the purposes of God, not his own.

Moses felt the burden, the responsibility to set the people of Israel free, but it wasn't until 40 years later that God brought the call to pass. After Moses had passed through the dealings of God, as far as God was concerned, that's when he was ready. When Moses thought he was ready, he wasn't. When he thought he wasn't, he was. The heart ambitious to lead is a poor foundation for great leadership. No leader should be too hungry for the job. We lead because of the call to lead, whether divine or human. In that climate, our motives are healthy.

A leader should expect supernatural power to accompany him and therefore allow room for God in his or her world. His providential hand establishes the chosen one. In a leadership contest, the man of God will find vindication from the Lord. His authenticity is established with signs from God. There are many with a message. There are many claiming leadership. However, those put there by God won't be trying to wrestle their position from others. Their security comes from above. The results will be self-evident. We don't have to drill into a tree to find out what it is like. Its fruit reveals all.

Absalom requests the king's permission to travel to Hebron to fulfil a vow he has made. This feigned submission for a pretended purpose is actually to stage a coup. He pretends conscientiousness when in fact his design is to dethrone his own father. He arranges for 200 men, innocent of the purpose, to travel with him. Absalom infiltrates the nation with spies who, at a predetermined time, will trumpet his enthronement. The city of Hebron, once host to both the temple and the king, has lost both to Jerusalem. Hebron's resentment provides the perfect ground for the revolt. Arriving in Hebron, Absalom invites some of his father's old friends to join him, even Ahithophel, David's trusted counsellor.

Ahithophel is the grandfather of Bathsheba (see 2 Sam. 11:3; 23:34). The pride and joy of old men is their grandchildren (see Prov. 17:6.) David, who had also arranged the murder of her husband, has violated Ahithophel's granddaughter, Bathsheba. Ahithophel sees his chance for revenge. He has left the capital for life in the country, six miles north of Hebron. His alliance with Absalom signals strong endorsement of the rebellion.

Each day the conspiracy grows. A messenger to David comes with news that the hearts of Israel are with Absalom. David calls for all his servants to flee the city with him. He neither wants the city harmed nor to be caught in a trap. Great military strategists know how to effect an excellent retreat as much as an excellent attack. Recall how after the Alamo, General Houston drew the Mexican general Santa Ana into his own defeat as the American general retreated day after day.

The most dangerous enemy is the one who is uncaring of position, power, or prestige and can forsake them at any time. David's view extended beyond clutching his throne and city at this time.

This moment is pivotal. Few of us realize how much destiny lies in the choices we make at crucial moments like these. Now everyone has to choose either David or Absalom. True loyalties surface. The result-oriented choose the side they believe will be victorious at the battle's end. Loyalty, however, knows no such choice. Whether we live or die, win or lose, we remain loyal to those God has called us to.

Finally David's men overpower Absalom in a ferocious battle that breaks out between their armies. The battle swings in David's favor and Absalom flees. As he races through the forest on his mount, the branches of a great terebinth tree snag his famous long hair. Eventually Joab finds him swinging in midair. The general pierces Absalom with three spears and he dies. His demise sends a sober signal to all those imagining that betrayal successfully seizes power.

Hushai joins David as he flees Jerusalem, but the king asks him to remain in Jerusalem and pretend to support the rebellion. Hushai, a loyal counsellor to David (2 Sam. 15:37), is to discover the plans of Absalom and relay them to the king through Zadok and Abiathar, the high priests left behind in Jerusalem to oversee the Ark. Consequently, Hushai, along with Ahithophel, is invited to Absalom's meeting to plan the next move against David. Hushai's advice is exactly the opposite to that of Ahithophel. His counsel favors David even though he appears to be helping Absalom. Hushai's counsel is accepted. David owes much of his ultimate victory to Hushai's inside help.

Zadok, joint high priest with Abiathar during David's reign, unites with David at Hebron after Saul's death, bringing 22 captains and 900 men (see 1 Chron. 12:28). His loyalty to David is solid, after being tested time and again in battle. As David flees the city, Zadok and Abiathar follow, with all the priesthood carrying the Ark. However, David directs them back to Jerusalem, asking them also to report all Absalom's plans to him, which they do. When the revolt is finally quashed, David calls on Zadok and Abiathar to arrange for the people of Judah to restore him to the throne. David wants his seat to be given to him rather than simply assuming it, so he arranges it. The tribes of Israel had made their choice for Absalom, but now they need to renew their choice of David. They reverse their choice without any recrimination from the king.

David's throne is reestablished, not by him grasping for it, but rather by his allowing the people to give it back to him. Even though he has every right to simply reassume authority, he arranges for the people to have their say and to give it to him.

Abiathar, the other high priest during David's reign, allies with Zadok, staying in Jerusalem to spy on David's behalf. He remains faithful to David during the rebellion of Absalom. However, his faithfulness evaporates years later when Adonijah attempts to seize the throne, and he sides with him as David is dying. Zadok parts company with his fellow high priest, supporting David's choice of Solomon as the next king.

Abiathar loses his position as high priest to Zadok (see 1 Kings 2:27). Loyalty must guide our choices all through life, not just at certain convenient moments.

Ittai from Gath (Goliath's hometown) joins David in the wilderness while he is a fugitive from Saul. Ittai commands around 600 soldiers. *Fausset's Bible Dictionary* describes Ittai's character as being of "unflinching loyalty, which David's misfortunes could not shake."[5] Following David out of Jerusalem, the king urges him to return to Jerusalem, because as a Philistine, he has nothing to fear from Absalom. Ittai refuses. Instead, he brings his entire family into covenant with David. Transcending short-term, result-oriented decision making, he swears allegiance to David in life or in death (2 Sam. 15:19-23). Regardless of the consequences, he chooses to be loyal to the man of God. Live or die, he cares not; he will remain loyal to David, the man of God. Leaders' victories are gained with these kinds of people.

Shimei, a Benjamite from Saul's tribe, claiming infamy, curses David as he flees Jerusalem. He resents that David of Judah inherited the throne of Saul, a Benjamite. He casts stones and insults and curses David as he leaves the sacred city. David's soldiers take action to kill him but David forbids it. He allows for the possibility that God could be punishing him. However, when David returns from the battle as victor, Shimei comes crawling to David in contrition with gifts, seeking forgiveness. Shimei is spineless, a stranger to loyalty, imagining the victory of Absalom was secure as he cursed the king leaving Jerusalem. Gloating over anyone on their bad day only invokes curses on ourselves.

Mephibosheth, Jonathan's son and Saul's grandson, is crippled in both legs. When his nurse heard of Jonathan and Saul's deaths at Gilboa, she fled the palace carrying her five-year-old charge. In her haste she accidentally dropped him. His legs were broken, never to heal. He is left lame in both feet for life.

When David comes to power, he scours the nation for descendants of Jonathan. He discovers Mephibosheth and invites him to sit daily at the king's table. He bequeaths all of Saul's vast estate to him and commands Ziba, a servant of Saul, to tend the land for Mephibosheth with his 20 servants and 15 sons.

When David is leaving Jerusalem, Ziba meets him with two donkeys and other provisions and informs David that Mephibosheth is remaining in Jerusalem, anticipating that David will be defeated and that the throne will somehow eventually be restored to him, being the legitimate descendant of Saul. Overcome by the arrogance and ungratefulness of Mephibosheth, David immediately transfers all the estate of Saul to Ziba, disinheriting the disloyal prince.

When David returns from the battle, Mephibosheth meets him with unwashed feet, unclipped beard, and soiled clothes, trying to ingratiate his favor. He claims Ziba has deceived both him and the king, slandering him as a betrayer. Not knowing what the truth of the matter is, David divides the land he had given to Ziba between the two.

How amazing that those people we help the most can be the least grateful and even betray us in desperate times! My experience is that the people who demand the least are low maintenance and always faithful in battle. Conversely, those expecting the most deliver little when they are most needed.

Joab, one of three sons of Zeruiah, David's sister, is the foremost general in David's army. From the beginning of David's journey to the throne, Joab proves himself valiant in battle and faithful through many wars. In a moment of dark intrigue, he even secures the death of Uriah the Hittite, Bathsheba's husband, for David. It is Joab who effects Absalom's return to Jerusalem and eventual interview with the king after being banished for the murder of Amnon. Yet, even this closeness to the prince does not compromise his fidelity to the king. He is the man who thrust three spears through Absalom who was caught hanging defenseless in a tree.

When David wants to number Israel, Joab, knowing this will offend Jehovah, the God of Israel, tries to dissuade the king. Unsuccessful, he is sluggish in carrying out the command, giving David time to reconsider and try to help him avoid the inevitable judgment.

After Absalom's death, David wants to reconcile the powerful armies that had gathered under the rebellious prince. He gives command of the nation's army to the two generals, Joab and Amasa, Absalom's general. Joab has a certain time to assemble the troops to place them under the government of David. Amasa lags in the task. Joab, deeply resenting the appointment of Amasa, finds the man and kills him on suspicion of further treachery.

Even though Joab was always loyal to the cause of the king, he never quite caught the heart of his leader. At one time David complained of Joab, "...these men, the sons of Zeruiah, are too harsh for me..." (2 Sam. 3:39).

Later, as David is dying, Adonijah, his third son after Absalom and Amnon, both now dead, believing he is the rightful heir to throne, gathers supporters. He declares himself king, even though his father David is appointing Solomon. Joab, having been ever loyal to David, at this point defects from him to Adonijah. Abiathar the high priest, faithful thus far to David, also joins with Joab in supporting Adonijah.

Adonijah's ambition is vanquished as Solomon receives the crown from his father. Zadok the priest, Nathan the prophet, and Benaiah the mighty man all remain faithful, installing the new king. Solomon commands the immediate death of Joab. Later he slays his rebellious brother Adonijah. Abiathar is banished to Anathoth.

Amasa, the son of another of David's sisters, has never received a command in David's armies as the sons of Zeruiah had. His resentment supplies the simple step into rebellion with Absalom and also gains him the coveted position of general.

David attempts to reconcile the man by giving him command alongside Joab, recently fallen from favor over the slaying of Absalom. His first task is to overturn a new rebellion by a man named Sheba. It seems, however, that he is unable to regather those troops under his command. Joab grasps the opportunity and pursues Sheba himself. He overtakes Amasa. Pretending to be his friend, he draws close and plunges a knife into him. Joab effectively removed all competition to his position.

Barzillai, an aged and wealthy Gileadite from Rogelim, supports David, who is encamped in Mahanim and hiding from Absalom. He brings David an abundance of provisions even when it's very unsure whether David will resume the throne. At this point, it looks more like Absalom will be victorious. People of integrity do not make their judgments on what they think the outcome will be but rather on what is right.

When David returns triumphant to Jerusalem, he invites Barzillai to live in the city with him. Barzillai declines the offer citing his age (he was 82). Instead, he recommends his son, and David accepts. Later, David also asks Solomon to care for the descendants of Barzillai. Our integrity and our faithfulness have far more reach than just our own lives and circumstances. Our family and friends will also inherit blessings secured from our integrity. Character ensures legacy.

Shobi, son of King Nahash of Ammon, and Machir, son of Ammiel from Lo Debar, are foreigners who also show David kindness, supplying provisions in his flight. David had befriended the Ammonite King Nahash during his sojourns in the wilderness. Loyal friends are one of life's most beautiful kisses. Our loyalty today returns to us tomorrow in desperate times. Unfortunately, the opposite is also true. Absalom's rebellion reveals that treachery today will return on us tomorrow.

So, what's the lesson? Unresolved offenses bring unbelievable damage to our future. Jesus repeatedly calls on us to forgive. He warns that unforgiveness brings demons, torment, sickness, bitter relationships, and a wall against God. Unforgiveness lies at the heart of a thousand and one problems we have in our world today. It's the foundation of so many problems we face. The answer is too simple. Forgive people who wound you. Forgive people who offend you before they say "sorry"! Even if they never say "sorry"!

The Bible has been saying it forever: Forgive one another. (Eph. 4:32).

Leading or Managing?

Some leaders should be managers and there are managers who should be leaders. Both need elements of the other, but we will be dominant in one of these roles. Leaders must have some management skills. However, a manager may not always possess the skills of leadership. Though leadership appeals as a better option for most people, it is certainly not more necessary.

Success in any organization rests on both management and leadership. Management people in leadership roles stagnate progress. Leaders morph into managers when they settle on maintaining achievements, instead of launching fresh ventures. The settled leader becomes bored. Their hearts beat for the front line, the new, and the bold. Leaders and managers are different breeds.

Any department of any organization needs a leader. The key to the success, growth, progress, and development of that department rests with a decision-making, problem-solving, inspiring, vision-casting, team-building, and goal-setting achiever—a leader. But every leader must have some management skills to remain viable. They must be able to get themselves organized, fixing the past, maintaining the present, and strategizing the future.

Each manager must have some leadership skills to implement the aims of the organization. However, it must remain clear who's who and what is required of each.

Here are some essential differences between the two:

Leaders	Managers
Vision-driven. Goal-oriented. Creates strategies. "Sees" the way.	Manages the process of achieving the vision and goals.
High communication skills. Inspires people to action.	Some communication skills. Shares information.
Makes strong, creative, initiating decisions.	Makes process decisions.
Gives orders.	Takes orders.
Pays the price of the vision in personal discipline and sacrifice.	Earns wages for work done.
Result oriented.	Process oriented.

Sets values and culture, out of which come policies and rules of operation.	Implements values and ensures conformity.
Builds a team through: • Selection. • Relationship. • Training. • Mentoring. • Including that team in his or her life.	Maintains the team through "climate control."
Unites the team through the great cause.	Prevents disunity by solving relational problems.
Gives improved meaning and potential to followers.	Help people sustain a process of improvement.
Less steady emotionally—susceptible to discouragement and angst. Requires high levels of encouragement from circumstances and people.	Steady, less flamboyant, but more predictable in responses.
Believes in the team and every individual. Releases people to do the job. Relates to people at all levels in an inspiring way, endearing them to the cause.	Manages by getting out of the way. Discerns the state of the team and the individuals. Comfortable with not believing in people and raising negative questions about people and circumstances. Manages by walking around; hands-on, close touch, creating the sense of accountability.
Believes the impossible can be achieved.	Assesses resources to establish feasibility. Best managers find ways to accomplish the dream rather than reasons why not.

We set ourselves up for failure if we imagine that our department will be successful simply because it is part of a successful organization. The success of an entire organization depends on the success of each individual department. The success of each department rises and falls on the leadership of that department.

In our organization, even though we may be considered success-ful, we have also had numerous failures. We have some areas that are propped up. We have other areas that are borderline in their perfor-mance and then we have some areas that are great successes. We have started a number of very successful churches. We have also started some churches that we later closed because they didn't work out. Every time it has been the quality of leadership that has determined the success or failure of these ventures.

The great thing about leadership is that it is an art that can be learned, developed, and improved. Paul tells Timothy to *"study to show yourself approved unto God, a workman that needeth not to be ashamed..."* (2 Tim. 2:15 KJV). Many of us get embarrassed because our results are just that—embarrassing. The good news is it's possible for us to learn skills to prevent this. Weak leadership neither gains nor maintains success. Therefore, we must identify weaknesses in our leadership. If you identify with any of the following eight shortcomings, decide today that you'll overcome them:

1. Weak leaders can't say "no."

Weak leaders hate to offend and therefore hate to say "no." Manipulative people can easily blackmail them emotionally. Strong leaders understand that the decisions that benefit most will also have a negative effect upon a few. We work to minimize the negative impact, but we also know it is inevitable that each time we make a big decision, there will be people adversely affected. However, this does not justify weak, decisionless leadership.

2. Weak leadership promises more than can be delivered.

Trying to win clients, associates, and employees with unfounded promises breeds disappointment and distrust. This places the wrong kind of pressure on the organization attempting to achieve unrealistic results.

3. Weak leadership fails to require.

That is, it doesn't set standards and then hold people accountable to them. Leaders are rulers. Rulers have rules. These need to be communicated to everyone. Good, realistic rules raise everyone's esteem—about themselves, each other, and the organization.

4. Weak leadership fails to confront people about their part in a problem.

Leaders tell people what they need to do to solve problems and accomplish the goals of the organization.

5. Weak leaders are easily discouraged by criticism and opposition.

Criticism is par for the leader's course. Charting new courses and breaking new ground always provokes opposition. Don't buckle at the first shot across the bow.

6. Weak leaders are easily wounded by lack of support.

Strong leaders determine to carry out their purpose no matter who or what is supporting them. This attitude itself attracts great support.

7. **Weak leaders are too insecure to recognize, develop, facilitate, and release other leaders in the organization.**

Strong, secure leaders celebrate the successes of those they lead.

8. **Weak leaders are feeble in personal discipline.**

Money, sexuality, relationships, time, organization, and learning all become areas of confusion for the leader who has never mastered self-control. Those who are out of control in any of these areas lose credibility, respect, and authority. Strong leaders realize they reproduce what they are, not what they say.

If we recognize any of these weaknesses in ourselves, we need to go to work on and strengthen these areas. If we're in a mess on account of these weaknesses, we need to decide today we are going to become strong in that area and focus on maximizing the leadership gift in us. Having weaknesses is everyone's lot in life. Overcoming them is the choice reserved for leaders. In the letters to the seven churches in the book of Revelation, John assures us that those who overcome will sit with Christ on His throne. Overcomers become throne-sitters. They rule and lead.

How about you? Do you have the patience, tenacity, and grit to bang the hammer of hard work against the anvil of your disadvantages until you've pounded your future into a shape that you like? Or do you just plan to sit there with your fingers crossed and wait for your big break; and then when it doesn't come, whine about how you never had a chance?"[6]

Overcoming weaknesses maximizes leadership, which in turn boosts progress and brings success.

Be diligent to present yourself approved to God, a worker who does not need to be ashamed, rightly dividing the word of truth.

2 Timothy 2:15

Leaders embarrassed about their achievements are not few. We either avoid discussing results or exaggerate them to give at least some image of success. Paul tells his protégé Timothy that if he studies to present himself to God as fit for the job, the success that follows will remove this embarrassment. This is also telling us that diligence in preparation enables us to equip others effectively.

This diligence is a simple process. It's about personal growth. It's about changing ourselves. It's about changing the way we do life.

It begins by meditating on those scriptures that deal with the character traits we need. We meditate on these scriptures until they are deeply ingrained in our subconsciousness. We read and listen to tapes on the subject until we become focused and see ourselves differently. We get with people who have what we want and learn how they do it. We see what we are becoming. Eventually, we find ourselves growing new skills from seeds planted deep in our mind.

Confronting

Jim Collins says, "Leadership does not begin just with vision. It begins with getting people to confront the brutal facts and to act on the implications."[7]

Confronting people over an issue is never easy. I don't know anyone who enjoys this. However, avoiding the confrontation doesn't solve anything. If we're smart, we'll choose our confrontations carefully. The culture of relationships with our team must be positive rather than a continual lecturing and correcting. The highest percentage of our contact with the team must be positive. Confronting people needs to be rare so that when we do it, it's accepted as serious. The petty person, always giving vent to personal annoyances, has evaporated his authority when he really does need it.

When we do confront someone about a problem, we need to tell the individual about our own shortcomings. Jesus gives us the strategy. Admitting how much we contributed to a problem is the first step in removing "specks" from *others'* eyes (see Matt. 7:3). It's also vital to have all the facts before we challenge a person about anything. If we have only half the story we will be floundering when they justify their position. Respect from the team diminishes.

> *Any story sounds true until someone tells the other side and sets the record straight.*
>
> Proverbs 18:17 TLB

Everybody tells their story to their own advantage. When we try to correct anything before we hear both sides of the story, we are doomed to fail. One of my worst moments in pastoring was when I was 23 years old and trying to look after a little congregation of about thirty people. A woman from the church complained to me that her husband wasn't giving her any money. He earned good money and they had six children. She vented about how difficult it was to feed and clothe her children each day. I was steaming! I marched to their house that same day and immediately tore strips off the man. Who did he think he was, coming to church, looking like a Christian, earning good money but not even feeding his own family? I ranted on for about 20 minutes with scriptures and rebukes.

When I was done, he asked me if I was finished. I replied that I was. He showed me the door, telling me to leave. As I walked down his drive I was saying to myself, "Something is wrong. He should have fallen on his knees, repenting. But exactly the opposite has happened. He's harder than ever!" I repeated to myself over and over, "Learn the lesson. Don't do this again." I'd lost the man. Now I needed to win him again and try and fix the situation.

Proverbs 18:19 says it is harder to win an offended brother than to break through the bars of a castle. I accepted this would be difficult but I believed not impossible. I went to his house again and knocked on his front door. He opened it and let me come in but said nothing. I sat in his lounge doing all the talking. He still said nothing. Eventually I left.

I did this every week for weeks. One day we were sitting, looking out the window, and I saw his children playing. I commented on how beautiful they all were. Suddenly, he began speaking. He pointed to the youngest child and told me that it wasn't his. But it was his wife's. She'd had sex with his own brother and now the offspring of his brother and his own wife was living with them. I felt about two inches tall. I realized why this man had withheld money from his wife. He was wounded with betrayal at the deepest level. He was struggling to come to terms with his own brother and his wife. He was ashamed, embarrassed, and cut. We talked. I asked if I could pray with him. We prayed, healing flowed, and he returned to church. There are always two sides to a story. Rushing to conclusions is the path of fools.

In confronting people, we need to accept the power of advocacy. People representing us always present our case more forcibly than we do. The saying, "the person who represents him or herself in a court of law has a fool for a lawyer," rings true. The kingdom of God, national justice systems, and the world of business all run on the power of advocacy. It isn't weakness to engage someone else to argue your case; it's wisdom. An intercessor (representative/attorney) can easily be more effective resolving our problems.

Whenever I can, I get someone else to deal with the matter (obviously there are situations where this is not possible—sometimes it just has to be you). This creates a much higher chance of resolving an issue without destroying relationships I want to keep intact.

However, when it is imperative that we ourselves deal with the matter, we should plan the time, the setting, and the words. Remember the prodigal in Luke 15 rehearsing his repentance speech before he made his way home to his father.

Organize a time when the person you are confronting isn't going to be distracted or under stress. Choose a setting that's not casual. Attach importance to the conversation by making sure the surroundings are not going to make it seem a small matter. If it *is* a small matter, then you simply need to deal with it within yourself, overlook it, and get on with life.

6

SOUND WORDS, SOUND HEART

Concerning King David, Psalm 78:72 NLT(96) reveals, *"He cared for them with a true heart and led them with skillful hands."*

In his research, Tom Peters reports that the best, most aggressive, and successful organizations were the ones that stressed integrity and trust. "Without doubt," Peters states, "honesty has always been the best policy. Divorced from ethics, leadership is reduced to management and politics to mere technique."[1]

Bill McArtney tells the story of the wife of a not too distinguished writer who once asked French author François Coppèe to support her husband's candidacy for a place in the French academy. "I beg you, vote for my husband," she pleaded. "He says he'll die if he's not elected."

Coppèe agreed to help, but his vote failed to ensure the writer's success. A few months later another seat became vacant, and the lady returned to Coppèe to ask him to vote for her husband again. "Ah, no," replied the academician. "I kept my promise, but he did not keep his. I consider myself free from any obligation."[2]

Leaders should be known as faithful and true. They keep their word. Trustworthiness is essential for any leader. However, we do not need to think that this compromises the possibilities for success.

Jack Welch is quoted as saying, "Excellence and competitiveness are totally compatible with honesty and integrity. The A student, the four-minute miler, the high-jump record holder—all strong winners— can achieve those results without resorting to cheating. People who cheat are simply weak."[3]

Character is moral strength proven to stay true under the fire of temptation.

Character is patient endurance when life is going badly.

Character is honesty at the price of punishment.

Character is reliability that calls for predictable behaviour.

Character is integrity in secret.

Character keeps promises even when that disadvantages you.

Character remains faithful to people you've made commitments to when it's not convenient.

Character stands firm on certain values even though it is popular to discard them.

Character lives by conviction rather than preference.

But character is not just moral prudishness that holds to unnecessary and unreasonably rigid standards. It also champions great acts of forgiveness and mercy in spite of the standards it holds to.

As leader of one of the western world's first mega churches, the Metropolitan Tabernacle in London, Charles Haddon Spurgeon, one of the great heroes of Christianity, taught his students on the need for character as ministers of the church:

A man's life is always more forcible than his speech; when men take stock of him, they reckon his deeds as pounds and his words as pence. We need indomitable perseverance, dogged resolution, and a combination of sacred obstinacy, self-denial, holy gentleness, and invincible courage. It is very ridiculous to hear good truth from a bad man; it is like flour in a coal sack.[4]

After the infamous Watergate scandal in the early 1970s, Charles "Chuck" Colson, President Nixon's "hatchet man," went to prison. Behind bars, Chuck met the Lord. His values, motivations, directions, and perceptions were entirely transformed. In 1997, Chuck spoke at the Australian national prayer breakfast at Parliament House. After being deeply involved in the most powerful leadership team on the planet and witnessing the horrific results of inconsistency between private and public lifestyles, he made the profound but often over-looked observation that public virtue does not create private virtue, but private virtue creates public virtue.

Republican Senator Dan Coates also offers some great insight:

Character cannot be summoned at the moment of crisis if it has been squandered by years of compromise and rationalization. The only testing ground for the heroic is the mundane. The only preparation for that one profound decision that can change a life, or even a nation, are those hundreds of half-conscious, self-defining seem-ingly insignificant decisions made in private. Habit is the daily battleground of character.[5]

The Bible lists the traits of people who lack character. Paul predicts that in the last days such people will abound. He describes them as *"...lovers of themselves, lovers of money, boasters, proud, blasphemers, disobedient to parents, unthankful, unholy, unloving, unforgiving, slanderers, without self-control, brutal, despisers of good, traitors, headstrong, haughty, lovers of pleasure rather than lovers of God…"* (2 Tim. 3:2-4).

The amazing point that Paul makes at the end of this dark list is that these people have a "form of godliness" (v. 5)—they go to church! They look like Christians. They appear to be godly but deny that God can transform lives. They are comfortable only with the notion of God, not the reality. They're okay with religion, but they don't want a relationship with Him.

Character is the foundation of our lives—bad character, bad life; good character….

Character is formed through habit. After repeatedly doing a certain thing for a while, it becomes natural to us. It becomes what we are. If we keep telling lies, we will eventually become a liar. We become deceptive, unable to live in the truth. However, if we develop the habit of truth telling, we become honest by nature. Character is something we can develop.

Robert T. Kiyosaki, author of many best-selling books on financial management, says,

> The liar will say such things as: "I didn't do that," or "No, it wasn't me," or "I don't know how that happened," or "Prove it."
>
> The blamer will say such things as: "It's your fault, not mine," or "If my wife didn't spend so much money, I would be better off financially," or "I would be rich if I didn't have you kids," or "The customers just don't care about my products," or "Employees just aren't loyal anymore," or "You weren't clear in your instructions," or "It's my boss's fault."
>
> The justifier says things such as, "Well, I don't have a good education so that is why I don't get ahead," or "I would have made it if I

had more time," or "Oh, I really didn't want to be rich anyway," or "Well, everyone else was doing it."

The quitter says things such as, "I told you that it would never work," or "This is too hard, and it's not worth it; I am going to do something easier," or "Why am I doing this? I don't need this hassle."

The denier says things such as, "No, there is nothing wrong; things are fine," or "Mistake? What mistake?" or "Don't worry. Things will work out."[6]

Our character is formed by our habits. Our habits are formed through repeated actions. Our actions come from our motivations such as desires, fears, loves, or hates. These are formed from our beliefs, our values. Success is built on values greater than success itself. Albert Einstein is reputed to have said, "Try not to become a man of success but rather try to become a man of value." If being successful is our guiding value, we will compromise those things that form character. If success is the value, a person will lie to sell something shabby. If honesty is the value, then a person might risk the sale through honesty; but he will emerge with a result greater than success. He is the possessor of integrity, character, and peace of mind. Plus, he will be trusted in his marketplace. This earns real long-term success.

Leading Badly

How terrible it will be for them! For they follow the evil example of Cain, who killed his brother. Like Balaam, they will do anything for money. And like Korah, they will perish because of their rebellion.

Jude 1:11 NLT(96)

The saddest tragedy in the world is to watch good people become bad. Yet, time and again it happens in both biblical and world history.

Many start strong but few finish the same. The highest goal we can have is to live faithful and true to God. Paul feared his own potential to become a castaway. He had seen colleagues fall (see 1 Cor. 9:27). We are engaged in the highest purpose in the universe, waging war against forces far greater than our natural selves. The enemy will take advantage of any and every situation he can to bring us down and prevent us from accomplishing this purpose.

With all the teaching on motivation, encouragement, and affirmation there is today, we also need warnings, corrections, and rebukes. These help us as much as, if not more than, the former if we're up to receiving them. History's record of bad leadership helps bring us a healthy respect for God and the determination to do it right.

The Way of Cain

Cain was the firstborn of Adam and Eve. In fact, he was the first person to be born at all. His parents were created, not born. His destiny was leadership. He felt the keen sense of responsibility unique to every firstborn. He desired to please God, but his passion evolved into dark motivation when he and his offering to God were rejected. He failed to understand that God's pleasure is in the person bringing the offering, rather than the offering itself. It's our state of heart rather than the state of our offering that pleases God. Abel came with faith, Cain did not (see Heb. 11:4). God's blessing falls upon the person, not on what he has to offer but on the condition of his heart. If the heart is right, so will the offering be.

Cain also failed to embrace followership as his basis for leadership. His parents, Adam and Eve, had relayed to their boys the importance of sacrificial offerings—and not just sacrifice, but blood sacrifice. They knew from personal experience that atonement for sin was through the shedding of blood, nothing else. Adam and Eve still remembered the smell of the skins that covered them, fresh with animals' blood back in the garden, but now a distant memory.

Cain's younger brother Abel tended sheep while Cain farmed the earth. If he were to bring an offering to the Lord, he would have to ask his brother for an animal. However, he just couldn't. He couldn't sing his younger brother's song. He couldn't speak his brother's message. He couldn't bring his brother's produce as his own offering. His pride wouldn't let him. He decided he'd bring what he wanted to bring. Shouldn't God be happy with that? But God wasn't. In the days following, the obvious blessing of God came upon Abel while Cain received nothing. Jealousy grew in the man. Soon this unrestrained envy turned to hatred, hatred so deep that it twisted into murder.

Cain couldn't cope with his younger brother receiving greater blessing than he, the elder, did. Even God appealed to Cain to humble himself, to improve his attitude and present a blood sacrifice (see Gen. 4:7). Cain refuses. He schemes Abel's death day after day until that fateful day when he ambushes and murders his own brother. Banished from God's presence for life, his ground struck barren, Cain wandered restlessly, marked for life with rejection from God.

All of us face that day when someone younger or less experienced gets more than we do. Unexpectedly, we find ourselves stretched, especially if, like Cain, we've always been first. When you're the one in charge, the embarrassment is not light. Those around you awkwardly defend your honor. Your temptation is to assassinate newcomers—maybe not literally, but at least to assassinate their character and dismiss them to insignificance.

What's the lesson? Bless the blessed. The promise to Abraham rewards those who bless him with blessing. Conversely, those cursing him reap cursing (see Gen. 12:3). To learn from the blessed, though it may bruise our pride, is the way of the wise.

What's the reason for blessing? If we're smart, we embrace it ourselves, fitting it into our context. Even Jesus flowed with his cousin, John the Baptist, at the river Jordan. He made John baptize Him just like everyone else (see Matt. 3:13). He began preaching the message John was preaching (see Matt. 4:17). He began baptizing just as John did (see John 3:22). Jesus' ministry emerged not in reaction to John but in submission to it. Jesus passed from followership to leadership and the awesome purpose of his life began to unfold.

The Greed of Balaam

Balaam represents those leaders who are so hungry for the rewards of ministry that they will sacrifice integrity in their lusty pursuit. *The New Living Bible* says, "*...they will do anything for money...*"(Jude 1:11). Balaam was gifted. When he blessed people, they got blessed. When he cursed people, they got cursed. He received inspiration from God. He sees visions of God when he "*...falls down, with eyes wide open*" (Num. 24:4).

Balaam was so effective that the Moabite King, Balak, fearing the advance of God's people, offered him serious money to curse Israel. Balaam knew this contradicted God's intention, but the lure of big money was overpowering. He treks with Balak to a mountain overlooking Israel's camp in order to bring a curse on them. However, he can't. His mouth can't frame the words. Instead, he blesses them. Balak is furious. But Balaam still wants the money, so he tries again. Again he fails.

He makes three attempts to curse Israel but cannot do it. He realizes he has no chance of cursing these people with words. They are

God's chosen. So the corrupt prophet devises a scheme to bring them down. He counsels Balak to send Moabite women among the Israelite men to seduce them. He knows fornication and idol worship will invoke God's curse upon Israel. (Num. 31:16).

Balak follows the advice of the reprobate prophet. Israel is corrupted and judgment falls. Although we have no exact record, apparently Balaam did get his hire. His eventual death was among the Moabites under the sword of Joshua

Now ministers should receive a healthy income from the ministry. The New Testament regularly lays down the principle without apology:

Elders who do their work well should be paid well, especially those who work hard at both preaching and teaching.

1 Tim. 5:17 NLT(96)

However, God has called and gifted ministers to execute *His* will, not ours or anyone else's. Using God-given abilities to oppose His purposes can only summon disaster. Neither our gifts nor we are for hire. Crossing that line where ministry is motivated by a lust for money only brings us into the company of Balaam.

The Rebellion of Korah

Korah's spirit is alive and well in the 21st century. Jealousy lurks ever near the ambitious who resent anyone else's success. How many times do we hear the words of Aaron and Miriam: Who do they think they are? They're just like us. We're equal to him (see Num. 12:2).

Christianity is easily misrepresented as an equalizer of everyone. Definitely, redemptively, we are all saved by the same blood and elevated to the same status as children of God, seated with Christ at

His right hand. However, as we continue to walk in His kingdom, differing levels of authority deserve commensurate honor. We will always be relating at three different levels of relationships:

1. Those we are responsible for;

2. Those who are our peers that we fellowship with; and

3. Those who are over us.

These relationships are meant to bless, guide, protect us, and to maximize our potential. Korah, along with Dathan and Abiram, claimed equality with Moses (Num. 16:1-3), repeating Aaron and Miriam's mistake. God didn't subscribe to the thought that they had some need for recognition of their value. He simply calls this rebellion. All of us who are committed to Christ would say we are obedient to God. However, this is impossible to measure until we have to obey people God uses to lead us.

Korah lured 250 leaders of the congregation to rise against Moses, meeting him at the tabernacle. They remained convinced of their position. Self-appointed leaders suffer the worst delusions. Beware of those blowing their own trumpets, overstating themselves. God blows our trumpet for us at the right time, at the right level, and through other ministers. Progression in His kingdom comes through endorsement by currently recognized authorities, not self-appointment. *"...Behold! The Lamb of God..."* (John 1:29), says John the Baptist of Jesus. *"He must increase, but I must decrease"* (John 3:30).

Korah and his rabble complained that Moses was making himself greater than all the others. Korah's opinion that he was equal is as old and dangerous as the rebellion of Lucifer. The fallen archangel declared he would be *"...like the Most High"* (Isa. 14:14). He too gathered a great company of angels, adding weight to his argument. The ground opened beneath the tents of Korah and the other leaders, swallowing them whole, along with their families and possessions. They disappeared forever!

> *Now Korah...with Dathan and Abiram...took men; and they rose up before Moses with some of the children of Israel, two hundred and fifty leaders of the congregation, representatives of the congregation, men of renown. They gathered together against Moses and Aaron, and said to them, "You take too much upon yourselves, for all the congregation is holy, every one of them, and the Lord is among them. Why then do you exalt yourselves above the assembly of the Lord?"*
>
> Num. 16:1–3

Reverence demands that we note that these were great men, men of renown, noble leaders chosen because of their once true character, who were enticed into a rebellion that cost them everything—their destiny and their lives. Only fools imagine that they are better than those before them. We are all susceptible to these exact same attitudes. Humility strengthens in us as we honor our leaders. Ultimately this is honoring God himself because we are respecting His choice. If we dishonor those He has chosen, we are dishonoring Him. If we honor those He has chosen....

The Arrogance of Diotrephes

> *I wrote to the church, but Diotrephes, who loves to have the preeminence among them, does not receive us. Therefore, if I come, I will call to mind his deeds which he does, prating against us with malicious words. And not content with that, he himself does not receive the brethren, and forbids those who wish to, putting them out of the church.'*
>
> 3 John 1:9,10

His name literally means "raised and nourished by Jove," which is another name for the chief Roman god, Jupiter, husband of Juno and god of light, the sky and weather, and god of the state and its welfare and its laws.

High achieving leaders inevitably have a healthy self-image, a robust ego. However, ego also needs a leash. The leader who breathes all the air in a room chokes everyone else out. This leader resents anyone else receiving any credit, attention, or privileges. Rather than releasing, he restricts everyone under his leadership. Let's call this disorder the "Diotrephes complex."

"I wrote to the church, BUT Diotrephes..." (v. 9), the apostle John explains. This leader is disagreeable. He's contentious. He's a "but" in the relationship. He's an opposer. John oversees this church. He is desperate to communicate with the people but the local leader is block-ing him. Never underestimate the power of leadership. It carries the power to release or restrict an entire church into or out of blessing.

"...Diotrephes,...loves...preeminence..." (v. 9). Diotrephes preens himself with the attention of the followers. The seeds of false pseudo-Christian cults are seen when leaders place themselves rather than Christ at the center of a group. They make disciples of themselves, not Christ.

"...does not receive us" (v. 9). A Diotrephic leader rejects authority over his life and resents others gaining access to those he has under his control.

"...prating against us with malicious words..." (v. 10). He slanders those apostles and other leaders who are attempting to bring guidance to the congregation. Slander is the signature of the insecure. It is the tactic of those who feel threatened, attempting to bolster their position by bringing others down.

"...he himself does not receive the brethren..." (v. 10). He is inhospitable, not only to those in authority but to any representatives they send. God uses the power of attorney. When we receive Christ, we receive the Father. When we receive Christ, we receive each other. When we receive each other, it is as though we are receiving Christ, especially if it is those God has given to lead us. When Diotrephes fails to receive John or his emissaries, it's as though he is rejecting Christ himself.

"...and forbids those who wish to..." (v. 10). Not only does this leader himself reject authority; he doesn't allow anyone under his influence to be subject to that authority either.

"...putting them out of the church" (v. 10). Anyone accepting the apostles comes under rejection themselves. John has written to the church guiding them into blessing. Diotrephes is blocking that. He wants total control and will not tolerate anyone expressing openness to the apostles to the point of ejecting them from the church.

Leaders who love preeminence miss the point of serving in the kingdom. They are buying into being a leader in a religious organization rather than a disciple in the kingdom. These self-serving leaders fail to serve people, effectively paralysing everyone. The result—no growth! Astonishing! Celebrating each other's successes in our teams should morph into promoting them into higher roles for higher success. Understand that one team member's success makes all of us successful.

A leader must engender loyalty not only to himself but also to those leading him and to the organization. Good leaders in a team draw loyalty not just to themselves but also to those above them. Every leader has been entrusted with the responsibility of caring for those they lead. Those above us have trusted us with those under us. We lead with borrowed authority. Others give us authority. We don't get authority by assuming it ourselves. Authority is given to us from above, from our colleagues and from those we lead. If those we are meant to be leading decide not to surrender leadership of their lives to us, we have no one to lead. It's important to remember that people are under no obligation to follow us.

In the church, Christ is the Head. Any pastor, leader, or ministry of any kind has authority only inasmuch as it has been given them. We don't take this authority—it is given to us.

Isaiah prophesies major secrets for abundance: *"let them stretch out the curtains of your dwellings"* (Isa. 54:2). This key unlocks growth for any organization. Unless we let them, the church will not grow. Letting them is releasing others to do what they are called to. It is giving permission. It is turning the responsibility for growth over to them.

Stephen Covey explains,

> We accomplish all that we do through delegation—either to time or to other people...Transferring responsibility to other skilled and trained people enables you to give your energies to other high-leverage activities. Delegation means growth, both for individuals and for organizations.[7]

Jim Rohn says, "You cannot succeed by yourself. It's hard to find a rich hermit."[8] Our growth depends not on us but on them. Leaders of growth free themselves from feeling it all depends on them. No captain anticipates scoring all the goals for their team. In fact, they actually don't have to score any goals at all! Great leadership manifests in captains leading their team to victory, no matter who scores.

Let me say again that any leader worth his or her salt has a healthy ego. However, this robust self-image needs management. Without a leash, a leader's ego can freeze everyone else out. Uncelebrated successful people leave. The organization atrophies. The key to great teams is a leader who recognizes, celebrates, and promotes his or her players.

7

UNCOMMON SENSE

Strength and courage sit comfortably at the helm of a list of required characteristics for leaders. But wisdom sits above all the other characteristics for the leader. Many strong, brave souls have been shipwrecked for lack of wisdom.

No one is intrinsically wise except God himself (see Rom. 16:27). All wisdom is sourced from Him. James exhorts us to ask for wisdom when we need it (see Jam. 1:5). All of us have said at some time, "I don't know what to do." If we do know what to do, how to do it can be just as daunting. Smart people never cease thirsting for wisdom. Depending on God for wisdom positions us to receive it. If we think we know all we need to know, our learning center shuts down. In a world of increasingly accelerated change where we constantly need to learn new things, this attitude is death. In his book, *The New Leaders,* Daniel Goleman observes that

> The act of learning is the key to stimulating new neural connections…Young people who work at mastering a discipline of any kind are laying down a neuronal scaffold that, later in life, will offer crucial support for leadership.[1]

Human brains can create new neural tissue as well as new neural connections and pathways throughout adulthood. At any point in life, neural connections used over and over become stronger, while those not used weaken.[2]

The brain's ability to sprout fresh connections continues throughout life. It just takes more effort and energy to learn in adulthood lessons that would have come more readily in our early years. We have to undo habits that do not work for us, and replace them with new ones that do.[3]

Meeting God is totally life transforming. The change is described in the Bible as from goats to sheep—from being difficult, cantankerous, swallow-anything people to gentle, meek, and trusting people. Jesus sends us, His servants, as sheep to the wolves.

Behold, I send you out as sheep [Luke 10:3—lambs] in the midst of wolves. Therefore be wise as serpents and harmless as doves.

Matt. 10:16

Sheep are symbolic of a trusting, submissive, quiet nature.

He was oppressed and He was afflicted, yet He opened not His mouth; He was led as a lamb to the slaughter, and as a sheep before its shearers is silent, so He opened not His mouth.

Isa. 53:7

Wolves are infamous for fierce, bold attacks. They kill more than they can eat. The taste of blood sends them into frenzy. In certain areas, shepherds recognize wolves as the greatest enemies of their sheep. The wolf is used regularly in literature to describe deceitful and greedy people.

Her princes in her midst are like wolves tearing the prey, to shed blood, to destroy people, and to get dishonest gain.

Eze. 22:27

Jesus realizes that for His followers to live like sheep, they are easy targets for the unscrupulous. So He tells us to be wise [cunning] as serpents yet harmless as doves. Synthesizing these three natures—sheep, serpent, dove— renders it unnecessary for us to become wolf-like to survive.

Jesus warns that we will have enemies and that there will be pain. Failing to accept this fact leaves us ill prepared for battle.

Therefore, since Christ suffered for us in the flesh, arm yourselves also with the same mind....

1 Pet. 4:1

Our battle is often dealing with our response to a world that uses totally different ways to "do life." With wisdom as our rule of life, we'll negotiate the worst of life successfully. One essence of wisdom is that we have the skill of learning, the ability to reinvent the way we do life.

Promising pain isn't rational when you're seeking followers, but Christ is unsparingly honest, revealing the challenges His followers will face. Great leaders are never afraid of declaring the cost of the vision. Garibaldi offered his soldiers only thirst, hardship, and death after the siege of Rome. Churchill offered his nation blood, toil, sweat, and tears after Dunkirk. Shackleton was overwhelmed with letters from volunteers to trek with him through the ice and blizzards to the South Pole.

Commenting on Psalm 23, Charles Spurgeon said "If we were without enemies, we might fear that we were not the friends of God."[4]

Even during good times, problems are not absent. However, we don't react to our enemies in the same way that they act toward us. We respond by the rules of wisdom.

Wisdom is not beyond our reach. Seeking wisdom is how we win her. Wisdom comes to those who thirst for her. Wisdom does not naturally rest within us. We gain her from elsewhere. Wisdom comes to us if we welcome her. When wisdom is valued above gold and sought above great wealth, she will be poured out upon us.

Wisdom is not a rule book. She is an attitude guiding how we do life. Wisdom gives protection. She rewards with favor, honor, and success. Being a believer is not a call to naïveté. Followers of Christ are not asked to be so trusting that we believe everything we're told. In fact, we are told to *"prove all things…"* (1 Thess. 5:21 KJV). Wisdom is to be knowledgeable yet not proud, confident yet not arrogant and not naive, but not cynical either, trusting yet not gullible, believing yet proving all things, courageous yet not foolhardy, humble yet not servile, encouraging yet not flattering, profound yet relatable, appropriate, being winsome yet uncompromising, righteous yet not self-righteous, disciplined yet celebrating life, prosperous yet not miserly, generous.

The apostle Paul speaks of this spirit of wisdom:

…that…God…may give to you the spirit of wisdom….

Eph. 1:17

Jesus himself was filled with this spirit of wisdom. A heavenly attitude clothed His life. In fact, the Holy Spirit, the Spirit of the Lord, is called the Spirit of wisdom. If we are walking in the Spirit, we are walking in wisdom.

The Spirit of the Lord shall rest upon Him, the Spirit of wisdom and understanding....

Isa. 11:2

Leaders must be wise in order to have a "whole of life" success. We are not wise without God or His Book. Wisdom is uncovered in Scripture. Our prayer, "Give me wisdom, Lord. Show me what to do," finds its answer in Scripture. Wisdom is the skill of living successfully. Wisdom wins.

One dictionary definition of *wisdom* is, "the ability to judge correctly and to follow the best course of action, based on knowledge and understanding."[5] Repeatedly throughout history, the teaching of sages, prophets, kings, leaders, and influencers points to wisdom as the key to success in life.

One anonymous proverb says, "A wise man learns from the mistakes of others. Nobody lives long enough to make them all himself." Wise people learn from the experience of others. Most people learn from their own experience. Fools learn from nobody's experience.

The Bible is rife with stories of people prospering because of wisdom. Joseph journeyed through slavery and imprisonment eventually to become second in command of all Egypt. Daniel survived the lions' den on his path to becoming advisor to the king. Esther became queen because of her beauty but saved her people through wisdom.

A scientist at NASA was assigned to prepare a presentation on lessons learned from bad experiences with the Hubble Space Telescope. At the briefing, lesson number one on his chart read, "In naming your mission, never use a word that rhymes with trouble."[6]

Doug Larson says, "Wisdom is the reward you get for a lifetime of listening when you would have preferred to talk."[7]

Automaker Henry Ford asked electrical genius Charlie Steinmetz to build the generators for his factory. One day the generators ground to a halt. The repairmen couldn't find the problem. Ford calls Steinmetz, who tinkers with the machines for a few hours, and then throws the switch. The generators are revived, but later Ford receives a bill from Steinmetz for $10,000. Flabbergasted, the tight-fisted carmaker inquires why the bill is so high. Steinmetz's reply: "For tinkering with the generators, $10. For knowing where to tinker, $9,990." Ford pays the bill.[8]

What we desire, we pursue. What we value, we seek. What we seek, we find or it finds us. If wisdom is that desire, that pursuit, then we will discover her paths, paths to succeeding in life. Wisdom is the skill to do life well.

Solomon, considered the wisest man in history, urges us that with all our getting of things, we should make the getting of wisdom the highest pursuit of our lives. He says we should elevate wisdom to be the most valuable commodity we pursue.

"Wisdom is the principal thing; therefore get wisdom…" Prov. 4:7.

Throughout the book of Proverbs, Solomon and other writers lay down that wisdom brings protection, security, healing, success, wealth, great relationships, progress, and growth.

Wisdom gains us favor with people who are important to our progress. Above this, wisdom attracts favor, not just with people but also with God. Wisdom opens doors that are closed to fools. Wisdom protects us from unnecessary trials, pain, and grief. Our appetite for wisdom must be high.

Many of our painful times are caused not by others but by ourselves. It's convenient to blame everyone or anything else, but this achieves nothing except to exempt us from guilt, which if we will just for the moment accept, will help us face the issue and make changes.

Wisdom Versus Foolishness

Contrast clarifies anything. Let's contrast wisdom with its opposite, foolishness. Here are seven characteristics of fools:

1. Fools say there is no God.

"The fool has said in his heart, 'There is no God...'" Ps. 53:1.

Atheism provides the convenience of freedom from moral absolutes. Without God, we are accountable to no one. We are free to develop our own values. However, whether or not we want it to be so, there is a God; and we will give an account of our lives before Him who gave us breath to breathe and a life to live. Leaders hold the fearful responsibility of shaping the mind-set of their followers. This means we are held more accountable than those who are not in leadership. Our authority has come from God above, not from us. We must influence those we lead to follow God.

Stanley Miller reports that Darwin thought that the cell was a simple blob of protoplasm. He conjectured that it evolved in a warm little pond. But as science continues to uncover the marvellous complexity of the cell, it becomes harder and harder to hold on to theories of chance. Biologists typically take refuge in the idea of endless periods of time. Given enough time, they argue, anything can happen. Over millions of years, the unlikely becomes likely, the improbable is transformed into the inevitable.

In the 1960s, mathematicians began writing computer programs to simulate every process under the sun. They cast their calculating eyes on evolution itself. Hunched over their (then) high-speed computers, they simulated the trial-and-error processes of neo-Darwinian evolution over the equivalent of billions of years.

The outcome was jolting, showing that the probability of evolution by chance processes is essentially zero, no matter how long the time scale.[9]

Atheism creates a vacuum of explanation for how the world works. Darwinism sits easily in this vacuum. The harvest of such anti-God beliefs, however, allows groups such as the Nazis to claim justification in exterminating millions of people, believing the evolutionary code of survival of the fittest to be right.

2. Fools mock at guilt as though sin has no consequence.

"Fools mock at sin..." (Prov. 14:9).

No one embarking on a sinful lifestyle realizes how expensive it will be, both here in this life and in the one to come. We live in a world where the word "sin" is dismissed as belonging to another age, as though this removes the wrongness of sin and its consequences. Only a fool scoffs at sin, failing to comprehend the deep problems that result from willful wrongdoing. History, including our present age, is full of landmarks screaming this fact. Only a fool imagines we can escape the inevitable painful clutches of a sinful life. It's impossible to embrace fire without being burned!

Charles Colson says, "The doctrine of original sin is the only philosophy empirically validated by thirty-five centuries of recorded human history."[10]

Colson sees rejection of the concept of sin as the source of the amorality of Marxism:

> The fatal flaw in Marxism's utopian view of the state is once again the denial of the basic Christian teaching of the Fall. If one is to believe there is such a thing as sin, one must believe there is a God who is the basis of a transcendent and universal standard of goodness. All this Marx denied. For him, religion and morality are nothing but ideologies used to rationalize the economic interests of one class over another. Small wonder that the totalitarian states created by Marxism acknowledged no universal moral principles, no transcendent justice, and no moral limits on their murderous brutality. The party, like the General Will, is always right.[11]

Colson also cites the example of the French revolutionary Robespierre who led the Reign of Terror in France in 1793. He agreed with the philosopher Jean-Jacques Rousseau in believing that in creating a new utopian social order, the use of force (including the condemnation and execution of those opposing the cause) was not only justified but necessary. This belief resulted in the imprisonment of 300,000 nobles, priests, and political dissidents, and the deaths of 17,000 citizens in that one year. As Colson observes,

> The utopian program of building a new and perfect society always means killing off those who resist, those who remain committed to the old ways, or those who belong to a class judged to be irredeemably corrupt (the bourgeoisie, the kulaks, the Jews, the Christians).[12]

Isn't it strange that all those leaders in history promising a utopian society inevitably bring hell rather than heaven to those following them?

With regard to atheist and French revolutionary Rousseau, Paul Johnson tells us that:

At the time Rousseau was writing *The Social Contract,* Johnson explains, he was struggling with a great personal dilemma. An inveterate bohemian, Rousseau had drifted from job to job and mistress to mistress, eventually living with a simple servant girl named Therese. When Therese presented Rousseau with a baby, he was, in his own words, "thrown into the greatest embarrassment." At that time, he was still trying to make his way into Parisian high society, and an illegitimate child was an awkward encumbrance. Friends whisper to Rousseau that unwanted offspring were customarily sent to a "foundling asylum," and a few days later, a tiny, blanketed bundle was left on the steps of the local orphanage. Four more children were born to Therese and Rousseau, and each ended up on the orphanage steps.

Records show that most of the babies placed in this institution died. The few who survived became beggars. Rousseau was quite aware of this unhappy fact. He knew he was abandoning his own children to almost certain death. In several of his books and letters, he even made vigorous attempts to justify his actions...His ideal state turns out to be one that liberates its citizens from troubling personal obligations. In particular, he urged that responsibility for educating children should be taken away from parents and given to the state...Rousseau struggled with guilt over his children...He grieved that he had "lacked simple courage to bring up a family"...People who follow a particular course of action are inevitably subject to intellectual pressure to find a rationale for it...Rousseau's story chillingly refutes the contemporary notion that personal morality has no public consequences. The world has paid dearly for Rousseau's personal choices, from the ovens of Auschwitz to the Game Temple of Synanon.[13]

3. Fools despise instruction.

A fool despises his father's instruction, but he who receives correction is prudent.

Prov. 15:5

Fools cannot hear anyone correcting them. They do not receive instruction for a better way. A fool imagines he knows everything he needs to know to negotiate life, not understanding that we travel through life successfully because of knowledge gained from others, often correctively.

Danny Guglielmucci, pastor of Edge Church International, formerly Southside Christian Church, one of the largest churches in Adelaide, Australia, says, "I need to caress people if I'm correcting them." Adding sweetness to our instruction helps people hear us more easily.

4. Fools enter too quickly into conflict.

"A fool's lips enter into contention..." (Prov. 18:6).

The wise are slow to go to war. Strife is not the way of the wise. Being angry with someone rarely fixes the situation. If we vent only anger, we strengthen, rather than release it. Anger doesn't solve the problem frustrating us. Self-control is more about controlling our temper than anything else. If we let this monster off the leash, it can effectively destroy our whole life. Most media and movies present the idea that the strongest or the most violent win. The wise know better. They know that a low-volume, calm response to anger will pacify. Doing good to those who attack us diffuses a great deal of rage.

The leader must be able to resolve issues without creating unnecessary conflict. Daniel Goleman, who coined the concept of emotional intelligence, has great insight into the power of angry emotions:

> Dissonance refers to a lack of harmony. Dissonant leadership produces groups that feel emotionally discordant, in which people have a sense of being continually off-key. Just as laughter offers a ready barometer of resonance at work, so rampant anger, fear, apathy, or even sullen silence signals the opposite...when flooded, a person can neither hear what is said without distortion, nor respond with clarity; thinking becomes muddled and the most ready responses are primitive ones—anything that will end the encounter quickly...when 108 managers and white-collar workers reported on the causes of conflict in their jobs, the number one reason was inept criticism by a boss. In short, dissonance dispirits people, burns them out, or sends them packing...people who work in toxic environments take the toxicity home. Stress hormones released during a toxic workday continue to swirl through the body many hours later.[14]

5. Fools are deceptive.

"...But the folly of fools is deceit" (Prov. 14:8).

Francis Schaeffer says, "Satan is the originator of The Great Lie—that we have the capacity, like God, to create our own standard of right and wrong."[15] It is a lie repeated so often that it has become the accepted wisdom of our culture.

The fool misrepresents reality, believing that he will get away with it, failing to understand that the truth we don't reveal will do so of its own force. The Christian is commanded to confess wrongs. This volunteering of truth brings wrong into the light, at which exact moment sin loses its power over the offender's soul. Also, the blood of

Christ has been made freely available to us to cleanse what nothing else in all creation can.

This forgiveness and salvation is offered by God himself. Only those choosing not to hide but rather to "come to the light" will find this unbelievably freeing force from heaven.

6. Fools fail to learn, even from bad experience.

As a dog returns to his own vomit, so a fool repeats his folly.

Prov. 26:11

The value of a mistake is that we can learn from it. The fool fails to learn. He keeps repeating the same mistake again and again. This kind of learning is not acquiring knowledge; it's simply gathering data in our brain. It is learning new ways to do life that we have not done before. It's relearning.

Leaders face the challenge of having to lead as though they know precisely what they're doing, while they are also learning along the way. The confidence of a leader should never morph into arrogance. Neither should a leader become insecure because he does not know what to do. The wise learn. They learn from those who know. A leader's responsibility is not to know it all but rather to have the wisdom to recognize what they need to know, to source that knowledge and then to have the courage to boldly implement it. This inspires those around them to buy into the action.

Jack Welch, respected as one the great business leaders of our times, said as the leader of General Electric, "Our behavior is driven by a fundamental core belief: the desire, and the ability, of an organization to continuously learn from any source, anywhere—and to rapidly convert this learning into action—is its ultimate competitive advantage".[16]

7. Fools are conceited.

...Do you see a man wise in his own eyes? There is more hope for a fool than for him.

Prov. 26:12

It's hard to not roll your eyes when someone talks as if the whole world were about him. ("That's enough of me talking about me. Now you talk about me!") People who consider themselves wise have closed the door on the spirit of wisdom. The philosopher Bertrand Russell (1872-1970) is credited with saying "One of the symptoms of an approaching nervous breakdown is the belief that one's work is terribly important." Former President of France Charles de Gaulle (1890-1970) said, "The graveyards are full of indispensable men."[17]

Wisdom Sharpens Us

Not only can wisdom be gotten, it can also be increased. Getting wisdom begins when we realize we don't have it. If we feel we don't have it, then obviously we seek this priceless gift. Wisdom sharpens us. She is likened to the sharpening of an ax, whereby the amount of effort is less than if you're using a blunt tool. Wisdom can reduce our efforts in achieving the same or even greater results—the greater the wisdom, the less the effort, the greater the results.

If the ax is dull, and one does not sharpen the edge, then he must use more strength; but wisdom brings success.

Ecc. 10:10

When we increase our wisdom, we sharpen our edge. Our cutting edge relates to our ability both to harvest and to build. The church leader must be effective in constantly building and reaping in the church. The essential harvests in church life are people coming to Christ and new members coming into the church. It is also essential to build up the team of volunteers and ministries and to nurture the growth and giving of finances. Wisdom provides the leader with the skills needed to accomplish these goals.

The cutting-edge plough softens the soil, making it ready for sowing the Word as a seed to be harvested. The cutting edge also builds. It fells the trees, shapes the wood, and prepares it for building the temple. Wisdom disciples people so they are built into the church. Wise leadership shapes people so they become effective as part of a living temple.

In order to sharpen our ax, we have to stop cutting. We sharpen ourselves when we rest. We lose our edge simply through work, through using that edge. Perhaps we used to have a cutting edge, winning souls easily, slicing easily through problems, easily cutting open the bread of the Word, easily connecting with God, easily carrying the burdens of leadership, easily seeing the future, easily believing God. Without a sharp edge, all this becomes hard. So we work harder. However, we find we're not achieving half as much as before. We're being set up for burnout.

We sharpen our cutting edge when we connect with people who take us further on than where we are now.

As iron sharpens iron, so a man sharpens the countenance of his friend.

Prov. 27:17

Men of iron (not wood) sharpen one another. The connection factor at leadership conferences is as powerful as the teaching in the sessions. Face-to-face encounters with other strong leaders sharpen us.

People who dull our edge disqualify themselves as friends. They are not helping. Recognize who your real friends are and grapple your soul to them. Friends sharpen us. You are more effective because of them. You accomplish more because of them. You are able to trace your effectiveness to their influence. You are more prosperous, able, and capable because of your association with them. These are true friends. Those who are not friends to your life leave you blunt, less capable, poorer, not richer, worried, doubtful, and discouraged.

If friends sharpen who we are, then our connection with them doesn't demand that we become like them. Wisdom accepts who we are, and we work within that sphere. Friends also accept who we are and help maximize us as we are. We must identify our friends (or those who are not) according to this criterion.

Wisdom is the edge that ensures the best kind of success, but she comes with a price. The price of gaining this edge is time. It takes time to sharpen wisdom. Then there's the price of recovering from failure, learning from what went wrong, the price of fighting the fight to think the right thoughts and have the right attitude. The lazy won't pay the price so they can't hold on to what they gain, because that which obtains a thing also maintains it.

A student in Elisha's school of prophets learned the price:

> *As one was cutting down a tree, the iron ax head fell into the water; and he cried out and said, "Alas, master! For it was borrowed."*

2 Kings 6:5

The students were cramped. Their living quarters were too small so they were building new housing. One student is using a borrowed ax, a borrowed edge, and he loses it. He seeks the help of the prophet and recovers it. What we pay for (rather than borrow) we will value. Therefore, losing it is less likely. If we have lost something good though, we need to recover it. A mentor can help us to recover what's lost. It's rare to recover a lost edge without someone else's input. Smart people will pay whatever the price is to get the wisdom edge.

The Nature of Wisdom

James lists lady wisdom's beautiful traits:

The wisdom that is from above is first pure, then peaceable, gentle, willing to yield, full of mercy and good fruits, without partiality and without hypocrisy.

James 3:17

Pure: She is unmixed, transparent, and clean. Wisdom doesn't celebrate the dark or the dirt.

Peaceable: She is unwarlike and non-provocative. Wisdom is a peacemaker, quiet, reconciling, calming.

Gentle: She moves slowly with a light touch; she is not heavy-handed but sensitive to others' feelings.

Willing to yield: Wisdom is not stubborn, cantankerous, or obstinate.

Full of mercy: She loves people in spite of their mistakes, wrongs, and failures. Wisdom is not accusing. Rather she covers others wrongs.

Full of good fruits: Wisdom is sweet, nourishing, and attractive, producing good results.

Without partiality: Wisdom fully accepts people without favoring one above another.

Without hypocrisy: The wise person's heart, words, and actions are integrated, consistent, and true.

The books of Job, Proverbs, Ecclesiastes, and James in the Bible are the wisdom books. A number of common themes are repeated throughout these books:

Learning

"A wise man will hear and increase learning"

Prov. 1:5

This obviously means a wise man knows he needs wisdom. As we have said before, wise people do not think they are wise. They feel keenly their lack of wisdom, thus seek her. The pursuit of wisdom is a life theme for the wise. The day we can say "I am now wise" does not exist. Wisdom means I do not think I am wise. She is ever my quest. The wise are teachable, always learning. Wisdom makes others her teachers. Because of this teachable attitude, the wise can learn from anyone and anything all the time.

Great leaders are perennial students. The art of learning never dies in the life of a great leader. The capacity to learn is by far more the responsibility of the student than the teacher. Even though we may sit under the teaching of the most brilliant communicators in the world, if we have no heart for learning they will teach us nothing. But if I have a hunger to learn, I will find lessons from the most foolish of teachers. Learning comes from hunger and humility. If we imagine we know enough, we have chosen to learn no more. If we decide we are in need of instruction, we remain open to learning more; and therefore we continue growing, changing, and maintaining relevance in an ever increasingly changing world.

"Anyone who stops learning is old, whether at 20 or 80. Anyone who keeps learning stays young," said Henry Ford, history's most innovative car manufacturer.[18]

Jack Welch once said of his company,

> GE is a bubbling cauldron of ideas and learning, with tens of thousands of people playing alternate roles of teacher and student. The operative assumption today is that someone, somewhere, has a better idea; and the operative compulsion is to find out who has that better idea, learn it, and put it into action—fast.[19]

International consulting firm Egon Zehnder makes the following observations:

> Openness is critical. We soon discovered how essential it is for a multi-business company to become an open, learning organization. The ultimate competitive advantage lies in an organization's ability to learn and rapidly transform that learning into action. It may acquire that learning in a variety of ways—through great scientists, great management practices, or great marketing skills—but then it must rapidly assimilate its new learning and drive it.[20]

Your teachability positions you so that regardless of your past, you'll acquire new skills, new knowledge, and do things previously not possible for you. Our brain is the finest instrument, the most advanced technology, the most able machine we have access to. It will accomplish the unbelievable for us if we train it to learn. We will never unleash its amazing abilities, though, if we ignore it by merely following unrestrained basic instincts. What could be worse than a wasted mind!

Brian Tracy says,

> The great breakthrough in your life comes when you realize that you can learn anything you need to learn to accomplish any goal that you set for yourself. This means there are no limits on what you can be, have, or do.[21]

Learning calls for humility. The proud can't learn. They can't admit ignorance and so they remain undeveloped. Humility recognizes its need for wisdom. Pride thinks it is wise. The Bible says the person who is wise in his own eyes is a fool (see Pro. 12:15).

> "He who asks a question is a fool for a minute; he who does not remains a fool forever" (Chinese proverb).

Possibly the most tragic biblical example of a man needing to learn humility is that of the great and powerful Nebuchadnezzar, who in just one day was reduced from a king to living in the forests like an animal and eating grass for seven years until he learned humility enough to declare that the Lord is God and source of all.

Paul the apostle says those who think themselves wise should become fools so they may become wise (see 1 Cor. 3:18).

Learning is not limited to the classroom. In fact, the greatest lessons any of us learn will be from life. This is because real learning comes from real life. We all make mistakes, we fail, we get beaten, we achieve. Everything that happens to us teaches us something if we want to learn, if we're intent on increasing our skills in life. We can learn all the time, all day, all our life. Make a list of major events, failures, victories, and mistakes in your life. What have these taught you?

In his book, *Rich Dad's Guide to Investing,* Robert T. Kiyosaki, the best-selling author on the subject of investing, says, "Life is a cruel teacher. It punishes you first, and then gives you the lesson. Yet like it or not, that is the process of true learning." He goes on to say that "a mistake is simply a lesson with emotions attached to it."[22]

There is an aphorism that goes: "I hear, I forget. I see, I remember. I do, I understand." The doer learns, the teacher even more so. Jesus tells us to go and teach the world His ways, to become His disciples. One of the meanings of the Greek word translated *disciple* (*mathetes*) is "to learn by endeavour." As we teach and do, we also learn. The more we teach, the more we learn.

The late Ed Cole, a founder and apostle of Christian men's ministry, said,

> Availability is not the most important factor in employment—teachability is.[23]

Benjamin Franklin felt that the best use of money is the pursuit of learning: "If a man empties his purse into his head, no man can take it away from him. An investment in knowledge always pays the best interest."[24]

We learn through various teachers. Mistakes can be our greatest teachers if we'll let them be. A mistake is not a mistake until we fail to let it teach us. The problem is never the problem. Our attitude to the problem is the problem—or the answer! It becomes a problem or an opportunity depending on how we react.

God First

The wise prioritize God in their world. We revere Him above all. However, worship is not true worship just because we place God first. When He is the only God we worship and make sacrifice for, then we have become true worshippers.

"Wisdom in Scripture is, broadly speaking, the knowledge of God's world and the knack of fitting oneself into it," says Calvin College professor Cornelius Plantinga. "To be wise is to know reality and then accommodate yourself to it."[25]

Solomon puts it like this: *"Notice the way God does things; then fall into line. Don't fight the ways of God..."* (Eccl. 7:13 NLT[96]).

Everything is surrendered to Him. No longer is our destiny in our own hands. We yield everything to Him. "God first" means He gets the first of everything in our lives—our time, our heart, our worship, our desires, our relationships, our money, our possessions—before anyone else does.

Solomon explored all the unbounded pleasures available to him, the broad strokes of life from laughter to melancholy, from partying to mourning, from leadership and power to servility and oppression, from wealth to poverty. He concluded that all of it is vain. His discovery was that the only worthy activity in life is to respect and love God above all else.

Work

Wisdom is not exemption from work. In fact, the opposite is true. The idea of the wise man being someone studying in an ivy-covered tower, pontificating in a cave, sitting and talking endlessly about unanswerable questions in discussion groups is stupidity. The wise are few in words and much in work. Yes, the wise work, and they work hard. Therefore, their achievements are not small.

The soul of a lazy man desires, and has nothing; but the soul of the diligent shall be made rich.

Prov. 13:4

Diligence is completing what we begin with steady, continuing commitment to the task. Diligence studies to get a full working knowledge of all it needs to know. Diligence is managing our lives with order, planning, and preparation. This makes success reachable. The lazy do not complete what they begin, having no idea of what their resources are, what state their finances are in, or the state of their business. Failure follows laziness. Success follows work. The only place in the world where success comes before work is the dictionary!

"Why did you leave your last job," asked the manager.

"Illness," he replied.

"What kind of illness?"

"I don't know," he said. "They just said they were sick of me."

Martin Luther understood the need for diligence in work when he wrote:

The maid who sweeps her kitchen is doing the will of God just as much as the monk who prays—not because she may sing a Christian hymn as she sweeps but because God loves clean floors. The Christian shoemaker does his Christian duty not by putting little crosses on the shoes, but by making good shoes, because God is interested in good craftsmanship.[26]

Work is its own reward. God didn't offer Adam a thousand dollars a week to be the gardener in Eden. To work the garden and reap its fruits were enough. Work is something to love. Work isn't something to avoid. It is something to embrace. It's a therapy all of its own. To work—and to work well—and to complete the job properly, and to feel the pride of a job well done all feed positively into the self-worth of a person's life. The lazy person whining about how the government doesn't do this and that for them, complaining that they've never had a break, sitting around all day doing nothing is slowly destroying his soul. The great life we all crave comes simply from working. Work is not something separate from God. Work is a calling.

> *This should be your ambition: to live a quiet life, minding your own business and doing your own work, just as we told you before. As a result, people who are not Christians will trust and respect you, and you will not need to depend on others for enough money to pay your bills.*
>
> 1 Thess. 4:11,12 TLB

John Wesley travelled 250 miles a day for 40 years, preached 40,000 sermons, produced 400 books and knew 10 languages. At 83 he was annoyed that he could not write more than fifteen hours a day without hurting his eyes, and at 86 he was ashamed he could not preach more than twice a day. He complained in his diary that there was an increasing tendency to lie in bed until 5:30 in the morning!

Wesley's published works include a four-volume commentary on the whole Bible, a dictionary of the English language, a five-volume work on natural philosophy, a four-volume work on church history, histories of England and Rome, grammars on the Hebrew, Latin, Greek, French, and English languages, three works on medicine, six volumes of church music, seven volumes of sermons and controversial papers. He also edited a library of 50 volumes known as "The Christian Library."

He was greatly devoted to pastoral work. Later in his life, he had the care of "all the churches" upon him. He would rise at 4:00 A.M. and work solidly through to 10:00 P.M., allowing himself brief periods for meals. In the midst of all this work he declared, "I have more hours of private retirement than any man in England."[27]

Luke 12:24 tells us that God gives the birds their food, but we also know He doesn't throw it into their nests.

Speech

A wholesome tongue is a tree of life, but perverseness in it breaks the spirit.

Prov. 15:4

The wise rule their tongues. Wisdom is prudent speech. The fool bubbles with indiscreet words continually pouring out of his mouth.

The mouth is powerful. Using it well is critical to a successful life. Success or failure is within our mouths. We are taught a thousand and one things at school, except knowing how to use our mouths properly.

Speech locates us. We rise or fall to the level of our conversation. What we say and don't say determines whom we get to speak to. If our speech is platinum, we will find ourselves among platinum people. Speech reveals character. Words reveal heart. All the strands of attitude, insight, empathy, respect, spirit, and knowledge are in our voice. People "taste" us when we talk. We're sweet or sour, loving or hateful, joyful or depressed. What comes out of our mouth impacts people. The tone, attitude, content, choice of words, pace, eloquence, appropriateness, volume, quality, pronunciation, knowledge, ignorance, joy, depression, spirit of the person—all are revealed through our words.

Wisdom knows what to say, and when and how to say it. She knows what is appropriate for the moment. Fools are recognized by their inappropriateness. The wise accumulate knowledge, but knowledge alone is not enough. Knowing how and when to use knowledge is wisdom.

Giving a good answer brings joy. It's difficult to estimate the value of something rightly said at the right time because it is so high.

The wise think before they speak. The fool says the first thing he thinks of and then talks on and on and....

A wise man's words are shaped not only by his head; he also feels the impact his words will have on the hearer before he speaks, and he frames them accordingly. He speaks with heart. He enjoys clear dialogue between his heart and mouth. The heart teaches the lips of the wise. We should speak at the pace of our heart, not the pace of our brain. Hearts move slowly, brains quickly. The brain has knowledge, but wisdom comes from deeper levels of our being.

Appropriate words and articulate speech are a fine art. There is a time for everything and wisdom understands the timing of speech. Knowing what, when, and how to speak is wisdom.

A leader's credibility rests on his or her words coming to pass. Unfortunately, it's too easy to let our egos predict the future. *"The wise man's eyes are in his head..."* (Eccl. 2:14). He foresees a future with his head, not just his heart. What we wish will happen and what actually happens are most often two very different things. Our predictions about tomorrow need to be sober, not intoxicated with current success and pride. If we are given to swelling predictions that never come to pass, we successfully undermine our own credibility. Better always to under project and over perform.

Regarding our credibility, it does not rest on what we say about ourselves. It rests on what others say about us. If you are to be recognized, let someone else do it. If no one does, don't attempt to do it yourself.

> *Do not boast about tomorrow, for you do not know what a day may bring forth.*
>
> Prov. 27:1

Truth always surfaces eventually. When it does and people know you claimed nothing of what you were due, your praise is just that bit greater (if praise matters to you). It is even better when a stranger rather than a friend praises you, because they have no vested interest in the relationship.

When praise comes, let it. Don't hose it down. Receive praise gracefully, crediting thankfulness and recognition to the team helping make the success. Understand we are not here to get glory. Our job is to arrange the adoration and glory to be directed to God. Wisdom sheds glory redirecting it to Him who gives us all things richly to enjoy.

Self-Control

The wise have rule over their lives because they rule their attitude.

Above all else, guard your heart, for it affects everything you do.

Prov. 4:23 NLT(96)

The heart is the believing machine of the human frame. Dennis Waitley speaks of our attitude as an internal thermostat. If our heart is sour, our whole life becomes sour; if sweet, then sweet. If we become fearful, doubtful, and cynical, our world becomes negative. Our relationships with God and people suffer when our heart becomes hard. When enthusiasm lags, our life turns down. We're bored with life. An unguarded heart is vulnerable so faith is easily defeated by fear, love by hate, and joy by anxiety. Unforgiveness is a toxic attitude infecting every area of our life; therefore, we are prudent to resolve offenses quickly, apologizing when we offend and forgiving quickly when we've been offended.

Location, Location, Location

The classic real estate sales maxim has a lot of other applications. Wise people position themselves correctly.

Mark out a straight path for your feet; then stick to the path and stay safe. Don't get sidetracked; keep your feet from following evil.

Prov. 4:26,27 NLT(96)

Paul says to flee fornication (see 1 Cor. 6:18). He doesn't say, "Stick around, be strong, and overcome the feelings." He simply says, "Get out of there!" Joseph understood this and ran so fast he lost his jacket (see Gen. 39:12). The wise are not found in places they should not be. It's just plain dumb to locate ourselves in places, relationships, or agreements that compromise our values. We simply don't go to the pornographic website, the "gentleman's club," the party where temptation is everywhere, or the table where drunkenness is normal. We don't spend the night in a room with someone other than our spouse.

These might be challenging decisions at times, but they are all simple. The fool plays with fire until he is burned. The scars remain for life. If we have made these mistakes we definitely need to make sure we have learned our lesson.

Learning From Mistakes

It needs to be restated that our greatest teachers are our mistakes. If I can learn from a mistake, it becomes a priceless teacher. If I learn nothing, however, I am a fool. It has always seemed strange to me that the wise are not exempt from making mistakes. Even though a person is wise, they will occasionally still make mistakes. The difference is they learn from them. If I make a foolish mistake, learn from it, and don't repeat it, then I am wise. However, if I fail to learn and repeat it, I'm a fool.

Here some of the worst mistakes I've made and what I've attempted to learn from them.

1. Installing new leaders without consulting all the people affected.

When people are not included in planning discussions, they will almost inevitably have difficulties with the decisions that are reached. This principle became very obvious when I appointed a new leader in a very prominent position of authority in our movement. Even though I discussed the appointment with our movement's executive leadership and received their total approval, I didn't discuss the appointment with some of the more prominent leaders in our movement who are not on our executive committee.

The person that I appointed is a brilliant leader and walked through the transition with grace. Everybody quickly recognized his skills and leadership ability. However, I should have met with all the centers of influence (officially recognized or not) and discussed the plan with them. People's loyalties tend to be with the previous leader. To switch loyalties can seem like a breach of integrity. They had become accustomed to the previous leader. They had developed trust, but the leadership needed to change. It is vital to spend time with the team, easing them into a relationship with the new leader.

2. Trying to fix a bad attitude by giving people a position.

Another mistake I made in the early days was installing someone with a bad attitude, hoping that having the job would fix the problem. This person had complained to me that he had been serving faithfully, but he was now ready for a leadership role. It was true. He had been serving. He had been faithful. But now he felt there should be some evidence of reward, or a career path of some kind laid out for him. The concept was right, but the attitude was wrong, and I knew it. Against my better judgment, however, I made him our youth leader. I felt that he'd either mope around complaining to others, or he'd leave if I didn't use him.

He didn't lead the group at all well. He arrived late and unprepared for meetings. He was unsteady on his feet as a teacher and as a leader. He lasted only a few months, and we had to mop up all sorts of problems. He became embarrassed and more distant than before. Giving people a job hoping to fix their problem is doomed to fail. They must fix the problem before they get the job. Learn from mistakes!

3. Ignoring protocol downwards.

Once we have successfully installed a person in a leadership role, we need to respect the authority we have invested in them. If we ignore them and speak to people under them without referring to them, we incur serious resentment from that leader.

In a growing church, I have regularly found this difficult. Up until the leader is installed, I may have been the one issuing commands and giving directions. As the church grows, it's obvious one person can't do it all, so we delegate. But letting go can be difficult.

Most often it is simply the habit of leading in that area that we find hard to release. Yet, we cannot be above the structures we implement. If we ignore our own structures, only weak leaders will occupy those roles. The strong want to flex their muscles without being undermined from above.

We should give fresh leaders support and mentoring leadership. If we want something to happen in the music department, we shouldn't talk to the singers or the bass player. We should talk to the music director. If there is somebody we want to talk with directly, we should make sure the director is in the loop.

4. Trying to lead when you're too tired.

The most dangerous condition I've ever been in is becoming too tired to lead effectively. Twice I have found myself too tired to fight for my own convictions when the convictions of others have been strong. Both times have ended in disaster.

Soon after birthing our church, we started a school. The primary school years passed until the children reached high school age. It seemed a natural progression to start a high school. However, I had no sense at all that we should do that. I had appointed a pastor as the school's overseer. He had a strong vision for Christian education, and he had been very successful leading the school. In our board meetings, he argued the case for the high school with more conviction than anyone opposed to it had. Nevertheless, I had no positive reasons at all to go ahead. But neither did I have the energy for another fight to put up a strong reason not to proceed. One principle I live by is if I don't have a good "gut feeling" (witness) within, then I don't proceed. Yet, in this situation, the arguments I was presented with seemed overwhelmingly in favor of proceeding with a high school. So we did.

We didn't even make it to the end of the first year. After nine months of pretty well everything going wrong, I told the board I was repenting and that we all needed to repent for going ahead with something that God had not authorised.

Many years later, we eventually did start a high school, and it has enjoyed good success. The timing issue is the stumbling point for many of us. The "what" is right, but the "when" needs to be just as right. When I've allowed the decisions of others to guide the ship (when I'm not feeling it!), we've encountered trouble. The captain must be alert and strong enough to lead. If you are the leader, you are to lead!

We've always had a vision for television. Right from the outset of our church, we had a television program that today covers a footprint of about 600 million people and growing. A television station in our city became available for purchase. One board member was totally convinced we should buy it. I was unconvinced, but because this brother had been successful in other areas of our church management, I deferred against my own judgement to him. The purchase went ahead.

Suddenly creditors began appearing out of the woodwork. Bills had been unpaid and because we had purchased this station, we needed to pay them out. It seemed like money was bleeding out to nowhere. We kept being told that it would take only one more payment. Finally, I decided we just weren't going to make one more payment. It was a case of good money following after bad as far as I was concerned. It wasn't God.

Some of the money we had used was $350,000 a woman had given the church. Because it had been part of a divorce settlement, we had held on to it for a period of one year so that she could be sure that was what she wanted to do with the money. She had said if we didn't take it, she would give it to another organization. We'd even asked her to get separate legal advice before she wrote the check. Even after all this, she was adamant that she wanted us to have the money.

Then after another year, she suddenly wanted the money back. Both our lawyers and hers said we were well within our rights not to do so, but we chose to make that happen. My associate senior minister Simon McIntyre and I mortgaged our homes for the money to be repaid.

I had been too tired and too weak to fight for what I believed in. Today, I try to ensure my strength is intact. It's easy for the multitude of small anxieties and frustrations to wear us down to ineffectiveness. A leader is better served giving two hours a day to quality decision making than fiddling with a thousand small stresses for ten hours and then finding himself incapable of leading effectively.

8

SELF-SECURITY

...Run in such a way that you may win.

1 Cor. 9:24 NLT

As far as we're concerned, rich uncles, windfalls, and free lunches don't exist. Winners don't rely on anyone else to win for them. They win for themselves. They paddle their own canoes. They don't wait for others to do it for them. They do it themselves.

Losers blame everyone else for their failure. They are depending on everyone else for their success. "It's the weather." "The seed they sold me is bad." "The banker won't stand with me." "My friends let me down." "The other people in the church won't get behind it." "My parents won't loan me the money." "Nobody else gets involved, so what's the use?"

To win the medal, the athlete doesn't expect anyone else to train for him. To grow and sell the crop, the farmer doesn't expect someone else to plough, sow, and harvest for him. To stay alive, the soldier doesn't expect everyone else to fight his battle for him.

Abraham is the classic example of self-sufficiency, and his nephew Lot is the classic example of a loser—a man without personal convictions, personal drive, inner reserve, and resources. Abraham knew he was adequate in himself. His source was God. He knew God. Lot knew Abraham. He never developed his own line of blessing with God.

> *...Lot, vexed with the filthy conversation of the wicked.*
>
> 2 Pet. 2:7 KJV

Even though Lot's environment constantly frustrates him, he doesn't get out of it. Someone else has to rescue him from what he got himself into. He is living a compromised lifestyle, his soul restless with the world he has chosen to live in. He has no credibility with his own family. They mock him when he warns of coming judgment. The delivering angel has to literally drag Lot out of the city.

His wife resents leaving. Against the command of the angel, she looks back and her body is petrified into a pillar of salt, forever a lesson to the uncommitted. Even Jesus refers to Lot's wife as a person who was unfit for the kingdom of God (see Luke 17:32).

Lot is commanded to escape to the mountains. He pleads for a shorter distance, an easier escape, and a more comfortable run. This man couldn't paddle his own canoe even when he needed to.

His final days are spent in a cave. His daughters, fearful of a childless future, inebriate their father so they can have sex with him. The offspring of one daughter becomes the Moabite tribe and the Ammonites are born of the other daughter. Both tribes become perpetual thorns in the sides of Abraham's descendants, the Israelites.

On the other hand, Lot's uncle, Abraham, lives right, works hard, walks with God, trains his men for war, teaches his children the ways of God, trusts Jehovah, and prospers in life. This man, the father of the

Israelite nation, becomes a pattern for the people of God. He will be remembered forever as one of the world's great citizens. He is one of the truly great members of the human family.

Leadership is the call to govern others. This won't happen without the leader exercising personal management. This means exercising:

- Time management
- Mind management
- Emotional management
- Relational management
- Spiritual management

Have you found honey? Eat only as much as you need, lest you be filled with it and vomit.

Prov. 25:16

This verse relates to personal management because when we find something sweet to us, it's easy to overindulge. This applies even to religion. We tend to think that if a little is good, then a lot must be better. But throughout the centuries, most of the extreme wrongs done to others by Christians have been carried out by zealots. These are people who have not managed their God-life at all well, who have believed that if a little restraint is good then complete abstinence must be best. Their strange ascetic practices over the centuries have left a trail of dark representations of God and a harvest of misery among the people who have come under the influence of this religious crowd. It was such people who put Jesus to death, imagining they were doing God a favor. When the religious zealot Paul was persecuting

Christians, he justified his murderous actions by the zeal he thought he was showing for God.

Ecclesiastes 7:16-18 NLT is helpful to the fair-minded but completely abhorrent to the zealot:

> So don't be too good or too wise! Why destroy yourself? On the other hand, don't be too wicked either—don't be a fool! Why should you die before your time?

The apostle Peter finds himself in a very awkward position when God tells him to kill and eat animals forbidden to Jewish people by the "Book." He tries to be holier than God, telling Him that he is not about to eat unclean animals. But God rebukes Peter telling that him He has called them clean. Peter's religiousness has to be broken down so that he will accept the Gentiles, people he has previously rejected, all in the name of God, of course! (See Acts 10:9-16.)

Success is imperative. The alternative is horrifying. If we have any reaction against success, we need to lose it.

The measurements of success transcend mere numbers and dollars. Success is achieving God-ordained goals by God-given means. Our greatest success is in implementing God's plan in the earth.

Success is to love God with everything. This is the first command. The second—loving your neighbour as you love yourself—is its equal (see Luke 10:27).

Success is achieving the thing we set out to do. Success is discovering and doing what I am meant to do in this life. In his best-selling book, *The Purpose Driven Life,* Rick Warren says, "If you want to know why you were placed on this planet, you must begin with God. You were born by his purpose and for his purpose."[1]

Success is doing what you do as well as you can. Your journey is not just about arriving, but also succeeding as a traveler. Sometimes, success means I lose well.

Success can mean sacrifice and servanthood. Success is overcoming selfish greed and arrogant bullying. Francis of Assisi forsook his rich father's home and inheritance for a life of voluntary poverty. He succeeded in overcoming the temptation for political power and all the wealth waiting for him. He lived true to his convictions.

Success is forgiving when we want revenge. You should never be brought down to the level of a man who hates you by hating him back. Success is loving someone when you want to hate them.

Solomon said success is understanding that there's a time for everything and being in harmony with the rhythms of life (Eccl. 3:1-8).

Success is being patient when you want to rush. In 1 Samuel 13, King Saul is told by Samuel the priest to wait seven days after which he will come and offer the sacrifice ahead of the king leading his soldiers into battle. However, Samuel takes longer than anticipated and soldiers leave the battlefield. As Saul's fears increase, his patience runs out. He conducts the sacrificial ceremony himself. At that very moment Samuel arrives. Incensed, the priest prophesies to the impatient king that presuming to be a priest has cost him the kingdom. The price of impatience is not small.

Success is being confident when you're intimidated.

Success is being able to tolerate diversity.

Success is changing when it seems impossibly hard.

Success is beating a bad habit and forming a new, good habit.

Success is winning against yourself, doing what you should do, must do, but don't want to do.

Success is telling the truth when you want to lie.

Success is winning by the rules against the competition.

Success is endearing the favor of God over your life.

For me personally, success is leading a church and a movement of churches that are effectively reaching increasing numbers of unchurched people and leading them into becoming disciples of Christ. The call of God to me is to equip His people to provide the environment for this growth to take place.

God gives us as much as He knows we can cope with at the present, but as we "trade" with what we've been given, our capacities grow and we receive more.

Opportunists act quickly, without hesitation, not procrastinating. They are not second-guessers. God calls unproductive servants wicked and lazy. Even though it may seem unfair to us, the principle of the kingdom is that unproductive servants lose what they do have to productive servants.

From those who do nothing, even what little they have will be taken away.

Matt. 25:29 NLT(96)

Self-Image

People owning a healthy self-image have found the ability to synthesize honesty, humility, and confidence. We need to find the ground between Narcissus (the Greek god infatuated with his own reflection) and the ugly duckling who found no worth in herself.

The way we see ourselves is the way we'll be.

As [a man] thinks in his heart, so is he.

Prov. 23:7

Be honest in your estimate of yourselves...

Rom. 12:3 NLT

Make some short summaries of how you see yourself. Answer these questions with one-sentence answers:

Q. When I say my name, what sort of person do I see and think of?

A. I am....

Q. What is the purpose of my life?

A. My purpose in life is to....

Q. What is my personality?

A. My personality is....

Q. What are my capacities?

A. My capacity is....

Q. What do I think of my body?

A. I see my body as....

Q. What do I think of my looks?

A. My looks are....

Q. What do I think of my personal culture and lifestyle?

A. My lifestyle is....

Q. What do I think of my past?

A. My past is....

Q. What do I think of my future?

A. My future is….

This is not an exhaustive survey of ourselves but it helps us start to see whether overall we are negative or positive about ourselves.

Self-image is how we see ourselves. We become that image. The saying "The me I see is the me I'll be" holds true. We move in the direction of our dominant thoughts. Our imagination is a creative tool. We conform to the image we hold of ourselves. Our self-image springs from our having been created. We once were not, now we are. We are created beings. God, who created us, has imprinted His image into each and every human soul. We have been made in His image. His nature is the essence of our being.

> *God created man in His own image; in the image of God He created him; male and female He created them.*
>
> Gen. 1:27

*Roget's Thesaurus*says the word "image" is synonymous with projection, reflection, reproduction, engraving, true-to-life, and embodiment.[2]

After losing his keys, Patrick is looking for them beneath a street lamp. A policeman asks Patrick what he's looking for. "My keys!" he says. "Where did you lose them?" asks the policeman. "Down the road, but there's more light here"!'

The (sometimes mystical) search for who we are can lure us down paths without any real answers. We hope that others will help us to discover ourselves. But when others' opinions about us matter too much, we are like trees without roots. Our soul is doomed to a life of confusion when the opinion of others is our source of confidence.

...and they have no firm root in themselves but are only temporary ...

Mark 4:17 NASB

When we're happy with ourselves, we draw strength from deep within. We stop despising what God loves. I stop rejecting what God accepts—me!

A successful life calls for self-awareness. I need to know who I am if I am ever to begin getting comfortable with being me. This might seem unusual, but one step toward increasing your self-awareness is to get quiet and then tell yourself your name. Say, "I'm ...." If I cringe, I change the cringe to a smile. I get happy with my name, with me. Attaching new emotions to my name, I get to feel good about me. Positive emotions and my name are synonymous.

Our names are extremely important. If we're labelled "loser" enough times, we'll become dysfunctional. Label someone a loser and they'll act like one. Label yourself a winner and you'll begin to behave like one. Label yourself wise and you'll become wise.

God knows you by your name. Your name is written in His Book of Life (see Phil. 4:3). Your name is inscribed on the palm of God's right hand (see Isa. 49:16). God even changes our names as He sets our sights on a higher destiny. If your name is associated with failure, He changes it to success—not when it happens but before it happens. You see yourself as you will be, not as you are now. You name yourself as you will be, not as you are now.

Abram, 75 years old and childless, has his name changed by God to Abraham. He accepts this. He begins signing his name Abraham, meaning "father of a multitude," before he has a child. God changes Abraham's vision of himself to something that doesn't yet exist.

My name locates me. Saying my name to myself, I remember those times I've been the unmasked me, the unself-conscious, free me—unafraid, laughing at breakfast, running through a field, swimming in waves, no masks, just me—and enjoying it! This is the person I love. This is the "me" I wish I could be all the time—the unself-conscious me.

However, this person doesn't seem to be enough. He's vulnerable, exposed, and unsteady. So we hide our true selves, emerging only when it's safe. We don't get the chance to grow. Cold rejection and mockery topple faint confidence, so we put on a mask of bravado, dying inside one more time. When the real me occasionally spontaneously skips out, I'm taken by surprise. I shock myself. My follow-up emotions aren't strong enough and I laugh at my own expression, grind my teeth, cringe inside, and look at the floor, embarrassed, dying again. The memory pinches and I kick the door.

But change is happening. Who I am is fine. I refuse to be embarrassed about what God is totally unashamed of. I learn to accept the "me" I am. What I say is as valuable as what others say. If I'm short on knowledge, I don't say anything. I don't have to. I know in myself I'm enough. I don't have to prove it. If I see myself through the eyes of others, they will always be giants with a better everything than me, and I'll be just a grasshopper.

> There also we saw the Nephilim (the sons of Anak are part of the Nephilim); and we became like grasshoppers in our own sight, and so we were in their sight.
>
> Num. 13:33 NASB

The underdog mind-set of the Hebrew slaves evaporates their abilities when they see themselves through the eyes of their enemy.

They see themselves as grasshoppers. In contrast, champions see themselves through the eyes of God. He sees them winning so they see themselves winning. Champions return an unembarrassed thank you to compliments.

Susan Jeffers, PhD, author, and sought-after public speaker, says

I spent 10 years studying psychology. But the most powerful principle I know about the human mind, I learned much later. Speaking positive words makes us mentally and physically strong, negative words make us weak—whether or not we believe the words as we speak them...[The] inner self doesn't know what is true and false; it believes what it is told. Our fearful chatterbox must be out-talked.[3]

The people who believe they are failures find it hard to receive compliments. It hurts. They just don't feel that good. We say, "The meal looks good." They say, "I think it's burnt." We say, "I like your suit." They say, "It's a cheap one I've had for years. The color doesn't suit me." We make down payments on an apology, not just for the meal or the suit, but for who we are.

But, hey, stop this today! You're all right! The meal is great! The suit looks sharp! Your preaching, pastor, is fantastic! Your business is exciting! Your art is stunning! Your music is wonderful! Your game is great!

Some search their family tree to discover their roots. What makes me who I am? Are there kings or queens in my heritage? If there are, I feel better about myself, more dignified. But what if I find I have a mob of criminals in my family tree? Once we receive Christ, our lineage is God the Father, straight from Him to me, a direct lineage to and from the nature of God. God has no grandchildren, only children, direct descendants.

We need to be products of our future, rather than products of our past. We need to begin behaving how we see ourselves in the future, rather than how we have been in the past.

The priests and prophets of our western culture—scientists, sociologists, psychiatrists, etc—tell us that our lives are preset by our past and that total change is virtually impossible. We are told our first five years determine our character for the rest of our lives. The logic of scientific findings argues that our genetic structure determines our personality. It's not a long distance to the conclusion that if we can engineer genetics, we can produce some kind of ideal race. Others in history have held similar plans!

We are also told that the traits of our father and mother will become ours. If they died of a heart attack, then chances are, we will too. If they had cancer, it is likely we will too. If they suffered from alcoholism or addiction, chances are, we will too. We are also told that our socioeconomic background is a major determining factor as to which side of the tracks our adult life will be lived on. We are also meant to believe that the stars, tarot cards, biorhythms, and fate have dictated a plan for our lives that is inescapable.

However, God has spoken:

*Therefore, if anyone is in Christ, he is a new creation; old things have passed away; behold, **all things have become new**.*

2 Cor. 5:17

Undoubtedly, some of those things mentioned above do influence us, but we do not have to accept them as the primary shapers of who we are. Romans 5:17 says those who live in Christ will rule in life. If Christ rules in our heart, we rule in this life. The major result of the Holy

Spirit coming into our life is the ability to recover self-control over our thoughts, emotions, attitudes, bodies, circumstances, and relationships.

The moment we receive Christ, God becomes our Father, and we become His children. Your family tree changes! You inherit His character traits. He has never been an alcoholic, has never had cancer, and He has never died of a heart attack. He has remained in extremely good health for an extremely long time! In fact, He has never been sick and never will be!

The minute you receive Christ, you inherit the nature of the Almighty God. Your socioeconomic background is translated from earth to heaven. You have become a member of the family of God! Noah, Abraham, and Paul the apostle are among those who are your family! Jesus himself is your brother.

Heaven is neither poor nor lacking anything. Those who seek the Lord shall not lack any good thing (see Ps. 34:10). Our socioeconomic background is completely transformed. Our natural genetic structure need no longer determine who we are. The major influence upon our life is the Holy Spirit. Our spirit has been recreated in the image of God. We are filled with the genes, the mighty power, of the Holy Spirit. Our first five years no longer control us. We are born again.

God's opinion of us is all-important because His statements regarding us are truth, not just facts. The truth is we're the image of God in the earth. It gets a little blurred at times. But we are His image in His earth. You are joyful, happy, and a picture of health itself. You are creative, confident, forgiving, compassionate, merciful, and kind. You are patient and triumphant. For you, life is good. With Christ and His image in you, not even death can keep you down. You have life, resurrection life, in you.

Self-image is our internal climate controller. Turn it up and our whole life turns up. Turn it down and…. We live out the way we are inside.

When I change, I tell others who this new person is. And now the new "me" that I've become enables me do what I do. I am the master and my mind the servant. Even though we can be held captive by impressions from the past shaping our lives, change takes place when *I* decide who I am rather than those voices from the past. Changing a self-image means I blow up the old, unwanted, misguided, underrated image of myself—it goes. I close my eyes. I see myself as a different person. He's a successful, winning champion. He gets what he aims for, again and again. Gradually, this new image replaces the old. This is the process of appropriating truth into fact. God does this with Abraham, Jacob, Peter, and Paul. He shows them what they can become. They see it. Their minds fasten on the target. Autopilot *on!* Our job is to keep the target on the screen. We are like a heat-seeking missile—the picture that's hot claims our attention. We move toward the event that turns us on, the thing that lights our fire. We move through life and hit our bull's-eye, because that's the way life works.

Winners make it happen. Losers let it happen

We all, with unveiled face, beholding as in a mirror the glory of the Lord, are being transformed into the same image from glory to glory …

2 Cor. 3:18

Self-Respect

If I respect who I am, I live above my animal instincts—the flesh, the lower nature, the old man, the carnal nature. The force called "sin" resident in my flesh pushes me to do things that I hate myself for afterwards. Then I direct my hate outward towards others. Amnon, a son of King David, is in love with his sister Tamar. Unbelievably, he rapes her. He is a king's son on the outside, but not on the inside. Inside he's a slave, ruled by lust he can't control. After the torrid moment, he hates himself and his wasted sister. "Get out of here," he tells the woman over whom just minutes before he had been "sick with love" (2 Sam. 13:14-16).

The moth is attracted to the light of the fire, but the fire will kill it. It's not the heat, but the light that is seemingly irresistible. A hot room doesn't attract moths. As the moth circles ever closer, unable to resist the attraction, it is finally burned to death. All of us face the same dilemma. We are attracted to things that will destroy us, and unless we make strong choices to live above the temptations, they will destroy us. God has left us with options, so that we will make choices that honor Him. And as a result, we lift our own lives.

Self-respect demands discipline that keeps us within certain boundaries. Living as a king's son should keep me above the downward pull.

The law of the Spirit of life in Christ Jesus has made me free from the law of sin and death.

Rom. 8:2

One law overcomes another. Gravity is an all powerful, pervasive law of the universe. However, the law of aerodynamics overcomes the law of gravity. The wing with its aerodynamic shaping lifts the aeroplane as it jets forward. It defeats gravity. Sin, negativity, and the world are powerful forces. However, the resurrection power of Jesus Christ lifts me above those laws. We choose to live by different rules and find ourselves powered from within.

Because I respect who I am, I am not intimidated. I don't need to be patronised. I can laugh at myself. I'm okay with being me. I can be self-effacing because I'm secure, deep inside. I don't have to humiliate others to establish my place. I don't get second chances at first impressions, so I look my best and look you in the eye; and we both feel good with a firm handshake. After only six seconds, we each have an opinion about the other. Others treat us like royalty because that's what we are inside—children of a King.

This self-respect causes me to live life right. I speak well. I leave out certain words because of what is good and acceptable to me and what is not. I choose right out of respect for who I am. I refuse to corrupt this person made in the image of God. The amazing outcome of this is the respect I receive from others. If we respect ourselves, others will too. If we accept ourselves, others will too. Maybe the reason we don't receive the respect we desire is because we fail to give it to ourselves.

A further outcome is that because we respect who we are, we easily show respect to others. These are basic life skills Jesus taught when He said we are to love others as ourselves, and do to others as we'd have done to us (see Matt. 19:19).

The heart of the problem is generally the problem of the heart. Deep inside, I need to enjoy being me. I have to take me with me everywhere I go. I can catch a plane to Greece, go to a disco, become a millionaire, or swallow some pills, trying to be someone else somewhere else, but I will find that I'm there too. I, just as I am, will be with me everywhere I go. I have got to stop trying to escape myself and start enjoying being who God has made me.

Self-Esteem

"Victimitis" robs us of faith that overcomes. It robs us of the "I believe I can do it" mind-set. People defeat themselves before they even begin. For six weeks the entire Israelite army is paralyzed with fear as Goliath the giant roars his reverberating challenge through the valley, "Give me a man!" Not one soldier is thinking outside the norms of warfare. Their world is frozen. Yet one young shepherd, without a uniform, without armour, without any combat experience, without sword or spear believes he can do it. Inside, he is a warrior. He sees himself winning. He sees himself equal to the giant.

We esteem ourselves capable because we know that "*...with God all things are possible*" (Matt. 19:26). We know that we "*...can do all things through Christ who strengthens [us]*" (Phil. 4:13). We know that nothing is impossible to him who believes (see Matt. 17:20).

David Yonggi Cho, Pastor of the Full Gospel Central Church in Seoul, Korea, with a congregation of 800,000, elevates self-esteem, discipline, and the vision of the church leader as central factors in the growth of a church.

Self-esteem can be boosted by our education, our talents, our background, our heritage, our house, our car, etc, but it shouldn't be founded on such things. These help, but they are certainly not the bottom line. The bottom line is me and the fact that I'm confident about being me. How many talented failures have you met? How many doctoral disasters do you know? If I'm confident that I can do something, then my self-teaching abilities will be harnessed, my self-learning capacities unleashed, and I will acquire the intelligence and education, or the talent I need to take me on a path to success. It all comes together because I believe I can do it. I rise to what I believe about myself. I become what I believed I could be. That vision God shows me—the vision of me being like Him.

A study by Harvard University reveals that 85 percent of the reasons for success—accomplishments, promotions, etc.—are to do with attitude, while technical expertise and ability only account for 15 percent.[4]

The business, entertainment, and sporting worlds reveal a definite pattern of the successful person—they're successful inside first. The successful person has purpose burning inside for their world. They are competent and organized. Their speech is effective. They communicate simply (using less instead of more), briefly (not taking a long time), specifically (sticking to the point), and clearly (ensuring no misunderstandings). They ask more than they tell (Could it be that…?; Would you think…?; Is it possible that…?). These people listen to answers, making sure they understand, not accepting generalities. Successful people remain calm under pressure. They don't rush. They are decisive, stating the problem, then the solution, talking straight, not wasting time.

These people are confident. Obstacles are opportunities. They're not tense with their superiors or anyone else. They're easy with the art of casual conversation. They dress one level up, keeping weight down.

There are unspoken rules to living successfully. They are obvious. Those disregarding them shouldn't wonder why they keep losing.

Self-Worth

When we believe we have worth to God and others, then we will live like it. Knowing our worth begins with the question, "What is my value to others—my family, friends, other people, and God?" Take a moment and write down your answer.

God uses people, not programs. When a leader says to me they have implemented a system and now it will work no matter who runs it, I know we'll be in trouble soon enough. I'll need another effective leader. I've actually seen it work the opposite way—weak system, strong leader, successful. Definitely there are methods and systems that are effective. But God has chosen to move in our world through people. He gives people methods to work with, but ultimately it is the person who is securing success.

Moses is told by God to climb the mountain and hold up the rod of God over the Israelite army (see Ex. 17:9). His army defeats the Amalekites in the valley below. However, as the battle wears on, Moses' arms grow tired. He drops his hands. Mysteriously, his army below retreats, defeated. He realizes the rod needs to remain aloft but he doesn't ask Aaron to hold up the rod. The power is not in the rod. It is in the man and the rod working together. Aaron and Hur help Moses by supporting his arms. Joshua leads the army below to victory. Victory dwelt in the man Moses, not the rod.

How do we measure our worth? "He's worth $50 billion." You've heard it. I've heard it. But God says "You're worth My Son." Our value in possessions, achievements, and dollars becomes paltry by comparison. However many billions and billions of dollars the rich may have, they still need Christ who has died for us all. He is heir and owner of the entire universe. He is the Creator of all that is. He is the ultimate "person of wealth."

In a world that values looks over most everything, it's easy to feel our worth is in how physically attractive we are. Plastic surgery is booming. The surgeon can take an ugly nose and make it seemingly perfect. Yet, after the bruising goes and the new nose appears, she can still feel ugly. Our perception is our reality. She has been feeling ugly for years. For outside change to have impact, our inside perceptions also need to change. We must accept that we are loved, accepted, and wanted by God. This is not just a piece of knowledge for us to digest. It is truth to be believed. Our value emerges from within.

*We have **known** and **believed** the love that God has for us.*

1 John 4:16

Some people need to win to feel their worth. Prior to fighting Michael Spinks, Mike Tyson, exheavyweight champion of the world, said, "I'm going to kill Spinks." Spinks was saying, "I don't even want to fight this man. But it's in my contract, so I have to." Ninety-three seconds after the first bell, Spinks feels cold canvas on his face. It's over. He was beaten before he began. People who win feel their worth before the fight begins. Losers fail before they start. Give yourself a break. Give yourself some worth. You're worth more. To whom? To the world, to your family, to the universe, to the eternal plan of God. You have value. Jesus says, "My Father looks after sparrows. You are of much more value than them. He'll look after you."

Do not fear therefore; you are of more value than many sparrows.

Luke 12:7

God sent His Son for each one of us. That's our worth. Our worth is measured by God's love. God's love places an ultimate value on our heads. How much am I loved by God? Did He send an apprentice angel, an errand boy, some unwanted cherubim, or a rejected human to die in our place for our sins? No! He sent His only, awesome Son, Jesus, the Perfect One, the ultimate Man, the Prince of Peace, who is in fact the Almighty God himself. For you and me. A gift from God to us. There's the measure of your worth.

Internal success is the first secret, the first law of external success. Life is lived from the inside out, not the outside in. And it's the inside first, then the outside. It's a law. Obey this and live!

9

AN EXCELLENT SPIRIT

It is God's intention that people succeed in fulfilling their dreams. The foundation for this success is an attitude of success. Attitude is everything. Great actions are born from great attitudes. The Scriptures direct a great deal of focus on attitude: "Children, honor your parents"; "Husbands, love your wives"; "Wives, yield to your husbands"; "Employees, serve your employers with enthusiasm"; "Christians, love one another; obey those who lead you."

Take a look at people with a bad attitude who imagine they can get through life without addressing it. As the years roll by, they harvest a miserable and bitter life. It's impossible to cheat the laws of attitude.

Daniel, one of the heroes of Scripture, finds himself promoted to one of the highest government positions in the land. Why? Because of his excellent attitude.

Then this Daniel distinguished himself above the governors and satraps, because an excellent spirit was in him; and the king gave thought to setting him over the whole realm.

Dan. 6:3

"Spirit" is attitude. When we walk in the attitudes (spirit) of God, we walk in the paths of success in life. "What" we do does not guarantee success; the "spirit" in which we do it will do that. Success is promised to those who live by the ways of the kingdom. This means I live within the boundaries of His Spirit. The kingdom of God is not geographical. Its borders are defined by attitudes. When we are walking in love, we are in the kingdom of God. This means we're under the dominion of the King, Jesus Christ. However, when we are walking in the ways of unforgiveness or hatred, we have crossed the border into the kingdom of darkness. We have placed ourselves under the dominion of the devil, and the world gains ground in our lives.

Attitudes are choices we make with the heart. The new nature we receive when we are born again is a nature from the Father. It contains the attitudes of God. We make the choice to walk in those attitudes. The power to live this way springs from the Holy Spirit. This is why it becomes so essential to be filled with the Spirit. He fills us with those attitudes that keep us in the kingdom of God. Our heart is the wellspring of our whole life. This is where attitude is expressed and felt. When we allow dark attitudes to dwell within us, we will be troubled. Great lives emerge from great attitudes.

Keep your heart with all diligence, for out of it spring the issues of life.

Prov. 4:23

Our attitudes determine our altitude in life. Christ determines our lives will be great even before we are born. However, He also reveals that the path to this great life is not the one taken by our world. He leads us to the same end but by the route of the kingdom. There is no censure over us for desiring to be first or to be great or to gain possessions and enjoy a beautiful life. He simply shows us a different way, His way, of achieving these ends.

Here are four things everybody wants at some time in life:

1. To be first

Whether it's first to get the prize, first in a line, first to be picked, first in a race, or first in a competition, all of us at some time want to win. Jesus tells us that anyone wanting to be first should position himself last or as a servant rather than attempt to shoulder his way into first position. Our need is to serve others rather than have them serving us. Notice though that He doesn't fault us for the desire to be first.

> ...Whoever who wants to be first must take last place and be the servant of everyone else.
>
> Mark 9:35 NLT(96)

2. To be promoted

Self-effacing people find themselves elevated, whereas those announcing their achievements soon have everyone's eyes rolling. In *The Power of Ethical Management*, Ken Blanchard and Norman Vincent Peale write, "People with humility don't think less of themselves; they just think of themselves less."[1] It's a law of the universe that if you put yourself up, you'll be brought down. However, if you humble yourself in any given situation you will find that people, circumstances, and God will elevate you.

> Whoever exalts himself will be humbled, and he who humbles himself will be exalted.
>
> Luke 14:11

3. To be great

Serving is the pathway to greatness in every field. Serving people is foundational to being successful. Any good business understands the culture of serving. Service is exactly that—serving. Hugh Mackay writes, "It is critical to genuinely care about each and every customer. If you want customers, treat them well. Everyone in an organization is responsible for customer service and all aspects of service need to be customer-focused."[2]

In *Made in America,* Sam Walton explains,

> "We're all working together; that's the secret. And we'll lower the cost of living for everyone, not just in America, but we'll give the world an opportunity to see what it's like to save and have a better lifestyle, a better life for all. We're proud of what we've accomplished; we've just begun."[3]

Sam Walton's dream was simple: give people high value, low prices, and a warm welcome. That dream was realized in 1962 with the opening of the first Wal-Mart. Today, Wal-Mart employs more than 1.8 million associates worldwide. The company has more than 6,500 stores and wholesale clubs across 14 countries. It has also expanded online with Walmart.com, which is dedicated to bringing Sam Walton's dream to the Internet.

If you ask customers why they return to Wal-Mart again and again, chances are they'll say it's because of more than just great prices and appealing selection; it's also because of the people, starting with the friendly greeters at the front of every store.

Al Neuharth, founder of the *USA Today* newspaper, drove around the country asking people what kind of newspaper they'd like to read. He took the time to stay in touch with the people he served.[4]

...whoever desires to become great among you shall be your servant.

Mark 10:43

4. To have things

Therefore do not worry, saying, "What shall we eat?" or "What shall we drink?" or "What shall we wear?" ...But seek first the kingdom of God and His righteousness, and all these things shall be added to you.

Matt. 6:31, 33

In a consumer-driven, materialistic world, these words of Jesus have never been so poignant. They strike at the heart of thinking that the believer should pursue a prosperous lifestyle as a priority. Actually, I have no argument with thinking prosperously. However, it needs balance. The balance is that "things" are not meant to be our preoccupation—God is! Jesus says the things we hope for in life will be added to us if we first seek Him and His kingdom. If we are always concerned with food, clothes, and housing, we are settling for a distant second, third, and fourth priority. Seeking the kingdom first assures us that "things" will be added.

Edgar A Guest writes,

Out of this life I shall never take,
Things of silver and gold I make.
All that I cherish and hoard away,
After I leave, on earth must stay.
Though I have toiled for a painting rare
To hang on my wall I must leave it there.
Though I call it mine and boast of its worth
I must give it up when I quit the earth.
All that I gather and all that I keep,
I must leave behind when I fall asleep.

And I often wonder what I shall own
In that other life, when I pass alone.
What shall they find and what shall they see
In the soul that answers the call for me?
Shall the great judge learn when my task is through
That the spirit had gathered some riches too?
Or shall at the last it be mine to find
That all I had worked for
I'd left behind?[5]

Seven Attitudes of the Great

1. Willingness

If you are willing and obedient, you shall eat the good of the land.

Isa. 1:19

Success begins with being willing. The willing-hearted find the way, the time, and the resources that get the job done. The unwilling find reasons why the job can't be done. Neither time nor resources are available for the unwilling.

The willing say "yes." The unwilling groan and complain, always finding a reason to say "no."

The willing have energy. Willingness breeds an energy all of its own. The unwilling are listless and fatigued. Watch children who have been told to clean up their room. Knuckles drag on the ground. They limp to their room, sit on the bed, and throw things at the drawers. Tell them you're going to Wonderland for the day and suddenly they have more energy than an Apollo spacecraft. They're dressed, in the car, and ready to go in a matter of minutes. Willingness releases energy.

The willing do the job well. They don't take shortcuts. They don't make as little effort and take as little time as possible. Even if you succeed in getting the unwilling to do the job, they never do it well. Impatient of good workmanship, they do it as cheaply and quickly as possible. They don't complete it properly. And once the sorry job is over, the cleanup is left to you.

The willing still battle on even when they are sick and circumstances are against them. Nothing is too hard for the willing. They believe they can do it even though it appears impossible. Faith comes easily to these people. The unwilling never have the faith for the task. They don't believe it can be done, finding all the reasons why not, thinking that explanations atone for excuses.

2. Confidence

...do not cast away your confidence, which has great reward.

Heb. 10:35

Henry Ford is credited with the saying, "Whether you think that you can or that you can't, you are usually right."

Confident, positive people succeed in life because that's where power is. The power of God lives in a positive climate. God does not live in the negative mould. He lives in the positive: *"God is light and in Him is no darkness at all"* (1 John 1:5).

Positive people succeed because they are attractive to be around. People enjoy brightness and warmth. People retreat from cold and the dark. We are drawn to the bright and the warm. A positive attitude is bright and warm. Positive people brighten a room. They lift the atmosphere.

The late Jim Cameron, a seasoned politician and one-time Speaker of the House in the New South Wales Parliament, attended our church with his family for some time. He was one of the strongest-spirited people I've known. His courage was seemingly indomitable. For many years, Jim lived with a pacemaker successfully lodged in his heart. Around 1990, he had a complete heart failure and was rushed to hospital. His only hope was a heart transplant. This was carried out within days. I visited Jim in hospital and was shocked to see him propped up in the intensive care ward with tubes and wires coming out of his body from everywhere. Small monitoring pads were attached to various places on his face and body. As soon as he saw me, he flung his arms in the air welcoming me to his room. Without missing a beat he said, "What on earth are you doing here, Philip? There are far more needy people you should be visiting than me!" Jim lived for twelve more years, the longest-living heart transplant recipient in our part of the world.

I have seen people with a common cold moan and groan, thinking they're about to die. The vision of Jim sitting up in bed with tubes everywhere, not complaining at all but rather possessing one of the most positive attitudes I've ever come across, will stay with me forever. He lived to see his youngest child graduate from high school. This is the power of a confident, positive attitude.

3. Humility

"I would have made a good pope," said former U.S. President Richard M. Nixon, who was impeached for his role in the infamous Watergate affair.[6]

Humility knows we need God. (Say, "I need You, God.")

Humility knows we need others. (Say, "I need other people.")

Humility recognizes how great we are not. (Say, "Lord, You've done it all.")

Humility admits our own shortcomings and congratulates others on their successes. Humility serves others we consider our equal or less.

Humility waits patiently. (Say, "I am patient.")

Humility restrains anger. (Say, "I forgive everyone who has ever offended me.")

Humility is not announcing our own achievements. Humility prefers others.

Humility is not something that is given to us; it is something we do to ourselves.

Humble yourselves *in the sight of the Lord, and He will lift you up.*

Jam. 4:10

Therefore humble yourselves under the mighty hand of God, that He may exalt you in due time.

1 Pet. 5:6

We humble *ourselves.* It's not the calling of others to do this. God would rather not humble us. He calls us to do it to ourselves. How? We choose the "lower seat" in each situation. Jesus says to do this at a dinner function. We serve at every opportunity. We get people their food. We take their coat. We open the door. We carry bags. We straighten seats. We pick up rubbish. We pull weeds. We help others with the menial tasks. We do whatever needs to be done. We even clean toilets....

Humility surrenders to God. We rely upon Him. We depend on Him for everything—for air and the lungs to breathe it!

Being "poor in spirit" is recognizing that we are inadequate and insufficient in ourselves. It's simply recognizing reality. We are not equal to conquering death, even less so life. Paul, one of the most competent and skilled leaders in history, reveals his own inadequacies:

I was with you in weakness, in fear, and in much trembling.

1 Cor. 2:3

At the Last Supper Jesus washes His disciples' feet. This work was always reserved for servants. Only the secure can assume a lesser role. Jesus is secure. He knows who He is. He isn't depending on recognition from elsewhere. The secure person has no problem humbling himself and serving others.

We are secure when, like Jesus, we know within ourselves where we are coming from, where we are going, and what we have. It doesn't matter whether or not others know. *We* know. It doesn't matter whether or not others recognize who we are. *We* know who we are. We can serve confidently. We humble ourselves without fear of losing in the process.

When we don't know where we are going, where we have come from, or what God has placed in our hands, we elevate ourselves rather than become servants. We position ourselves at the head table, we "big note" ourselves to others by letting everybody know all the big things going on in our lives. This is insecurity.

Recognition is something all of us crave. If we feel unrecognized, we seek it in ways that result only in embarrassment to us. Knowing that God recognizes us results in us not trying to get attention from everyone else. Strangely, when we are secure enough to be self-effacing, others will give us the recognition we crave.

Being secure sets us free to accept whatever we're meant to be. Servanthood is effective. Why? Because people are far more open to someone serving them than to someone trying to rule them.

Influence springs from a serving attitude.

Not that we are sufficient of ourselves to think of anything as being from ourselves, but our sufficiency is from God

2 Cor. 3:5

Humility is teachable, whereas conceit knows it all. Conceit can't be taught. Proverbs 26:12 says there's more hope for a fool than for a person wise in his own eyes.

My level of teachability is equal to my level of humility. Everyone can teach us something. We will never stop learning if we are not so arrogant as to think that we don't need to learn anything more.

Humility is not a servile attitude though. When we choose humility, we retain nobility. We walk tall. Jesus, the Son of God, the most humble person ever to grace the earth, says "I am lowly in heart" (Matt. 11:29).

"We are bound to be lowly, but our office as ambassadors should prevent our being servile," says C. H. Spurgeon.[7]

Humility is not inviting us to have a poor opinion of ourselves. To synthesize confidence, nobility, and humility is a lifetime pursuit. With God we can do it.

The self-effacing person will always be encouraged, appreciated, and loved by others. But the arrogant are in for trouble.

By humility and the fear of the Lord are riches and honor and life.

Prov. 22:4

Before destruction the heart of a man is haughty, and before honor is humility.

Prov. 18:12

4. Thankfulness

"...in everything give thanks..." (1 Thess. 5:18).

"Gratitude," said G. K. Chesterton, "is the mother of all virtues."[8]

In Psalm 100:4, King David exhorts the people of God to *"...enter His gates with thanksgiving...."*

In all but two of his letters, Paul the apostle first gives thanks for the people to whom he is writing.

"Blow, blow, thou winter wind! Thou art not so unkind as man's ingratitude," laments William Shakespeare in *As You Like It*.[9]

We live in a world trained in complaining, grumbling, and moaning. Our complaints have achieved litigious heights seeking compensation in the courts for things we should be accepting responsibility for ourselves. People with a gripe make it onto the six o'clock news. We are in deep need of retraining in the art of thankfulness at all times for all things.

*...in the last days perilous times will come: For men will be lovers of themselves, lovers of money, boasters, proud, blasphemers, disobedient to parents, **unthankful**, unholy, unloving, unforgiving, slanderers, without self-control, brutal, despisers of good...having a form of godliness....*

2 Tim. 3:1-3,5

These verses reveal that perilous times come, not because of the economy, not because of weather changes, not because of droughts, floods, or other physical trouble, but because of the attitudes of people. Included in the list that brings perilous times upon us is unthankfulness.

The disturbing discovery at the end of this horror list of bad attitudes is that these people have a "form of godliness"! They go to church! They act religiously. Being religious and going to church do not atone for stinking attitudes. The art of being grateful is awakening the heart of worship—to stand daily wide-eyed at the wonder of the world, to feel the awesome privilege of "being," whereby once we were not but now we are, births thankfulness inside of us. We are reminded many times, though few of us ever do, to "count your blessings, name them one by one...." Do it today. Count your blessings. Write and thank people for what they mean to your life.

Thankfulness is the air conditioner of the soul. It blows out the stale overheated air and brings cool refreshing breezes to the soul. Thanksgiving is the perfect way to be positive in life. Positivity without thankfulness engenders in us a hard cold triumphalism that feels like arrogance to others. Thankfulness includes God; we are saying His part mattered so much that it would not have been but for Him. Thankfulness to people includes others in the event so we are saying we could not have done it without them. Thankfulness reveals the humility that understands we are dependent upon God and others to be successful. Thankfulness is the key to the synthesis of a humble, positive, and confident attitude.

Fred Lloyd Cochran tells of a brief moment where he saw pure appreciation:

> Yesterday I watched a huge flight of geese winging their way south through one of those panoramic sunsets that colour the entire sky for a few moments. I saw them as I leaned against the lion statue in front of the Chicago Art Institute, where I was watching the Christmas shoppers hurry along Michigan Avenue. When I lowered my gaze, I noticed that a bag lady, standing a few feet away, had also been watching the

geese. Our eyes met and we smiled—silently acknowledging the fact that we had shared a marvellous sight, a symbol of the mystery of the struggle to survive. I overheard the lady talking to herself as she shuffled away. Her words, "God spoils me," were startling.[10]

In spite of all the difficulties you might find yourself in, appreciation and thankfulness will strengthen your soul to find a way through.

5. Serving

We've already spent a lot of time on this in the early chapters, but I find it impossible to ignore this in spelling out seven great attitudes of success. Serving rather than selling will bring a healthy success to your world. Jesus is better served than sold. Your product is better served than sold. If we can help people and serve their needs with what we are offering, then the "sell" is hardly necessary.

If we are committed to helping people get to where they want to go, they'll beat a path to our door. If, however, we always want people to help us get to where we want to go....

Robert Schuller said, "Find a need and meet it, find a hurt and heal it."[11]

Seek to serve others. Help them get what they want, not what you want. Help others get what they want at your expense. Sacrifice to help people get what they're trying to achieve.

Easily the most influential person in history, Jesus says of himself in Matthew 20:28, "*...the Son of Man did not come to be served, but to serve, and to give His life a ransom for many.*" He sought to give His life for the benefit of others.

Serving is the key that demands we humble ourselves and make the other person more important than ourselves. In the October 1992 edition of *Success* magazine, Jim Cecil says, "Love is nothing more than a massive liking." All other things being equal, your customers will go where they feel "massively liked" or loved.

It's just smart to look after people well. The enormously successful American clothiers Nordstrom keep file cards on customers' birthdays, sizes, and favorite colors. Coca-Cola managers annually stage a gala customer-appreciation week. A Memphis hospital has adopted a hotel model, using the term "guest" instead of patient.

Service will triumph over selling every time. If you serve people well, there's little need to sell.

The book *Good Service Is Good Business,* by Catherine DeVrye, reports that a survey showed that the *perceived* service industry leaders:

- Can charge 9-10 percent more for the same basic goods and services.

- Grow twice as fast as their competition.

- Improve their market share by up to 6 percent per year (while poorly perceived companies lose as much as 2 percent per year).

- Have a return on sales 12 percent higher than the perceived poor services providers.[12]

You can't argue with customer perception—perception is reality. In any situation we find the things that justify our perceptions, even when an opposing reality stares us in the face. All of us prefer to believe our perceptions.

Most disappointed customers (around 95 percent) don't bother to complain. They simply go elsewhere. No news is never good news. In a serving-focused business, we will go out of our way to hear complaints so we can fix them and serve our people better. As a customer, the feeling of being listened to and respected (or not) far exceeds the problem at hand. The fool assumes their client is with them for life. Other companies want them and are trying to get them right now. If we want customers, we must treat them well. Everyone from top to bottom is responsible for customer service. All our services need to be customer focused.

Back in 1993, Hugh Mackay, in his book *Reinventing Australia,* stated,

> Half the households in this country include only one or two people…As customers, they don't just want a product or service, they look for and value welcoming relationships. Individuals are seeking personal contact with those they deal with. Many people don't mind paying more for this kind of relationship, especially if they perceive it to be enhancing their sense of local community—a thing Australians perceive to be in danger of extinction and desperately want to re-establish.[13]

One of the smartest insights I've heard regarding serving is from Jack Welch: "A company cannot provide job security. Only customers can do that. One thing we've discovered with certainty is that anything we do that makes that customer more successful inevitably results in a financial return for us."[14]

If there were three most important things an organization must address, two of them have to do with serving people—the customer and the staff member. If these two groups are happy and we have structured good cash flow, it is a given that the business and organization will flourish.

6. Generosity

…a generous man devises generous things, and by generosity he shall stand.

Isa. 32:8

Churchill once quipped, "We make a living by what we get. We make a life by what we give."[15]

The generous person gives everybody a lot of room. His team attempts new things without fear of punishment for failure. They provide a safe risk-taking environment. The generous see a person's mistake as a learning opportunity.

A generous attitude overlooks faults. A mean attitude is fault-finding over the smallest of issues. Generous people are not easily upset. They overlook small inconsequential mistakes.

Generous people give more than is expected. They surprise people with generosity. They give without fuss, with simplicity, wishing they could give more.

The generous release others around them into success. In Matthew 10 Jesus calls His disciples to him and gives them power to go and do what He has been doing. Then, when they return saying they were casting out demons, healing the sick, and raising the dead, far from being threatened or jealous, Jesus rejoices that they were now tasting some of the amazing success He himself had experienced. Generous people don't restrict others. They don't just cope with others becoming famous and successful, they encourage it and help it happen. They are secure enough to bless others so they look even better than those in their field.

7. Obedience

Understanding, appreciating, and working with authority are imperative to true success.

"...the rebellious dwell in a dry land" (Ps. 68:6).

A person who would have authority must know how to be submissive to authority. Unrestrained power unleashes the worst in humans. Abraham Lincoln had a deep insight into this issue. Born in the backwoods of Kentucky in 1809, Lincoln worked as a rail splitter, boatman, postmaster, surveyor, storekeeper, lawyer, state legislator, and congressman before gaining national attention during debates for election to the U.S. Senate. When he was elected the 16th U.S. President, seven states had already seceded from the Union and would soon be followed by four more. He guided the U.S. through five years of traumatic civil war and issued the Emancipation Proclamation to outlaw slavery in the United States. His Gettysburg Address, written on the train ride to the battlefield, is still considered a masterpiece. He says, "Nearly all men can stand adversity, but if you want to test a man's character, give him power."[16]

The person who can take orders well, gives them well. In fact, it is said of Abraham Lincoln that he knew the value of making requests as opposed to issuing orders. The letters and telegrams that he wrote to subordinates are filled with suggestions, views, and recommendations; rarely was there a direct order. He preferred to let his generals make their own decisions and hoped that through his suggestions they would do the right thing.

Many surveys reveal that those who struggle with authority have trouble putting a team together and obtaining the kind of loyalty and obedience needed for them to enjoy high achievements. Those who have been enthusiastic employees carrying out directives without atti- tude and not having issues with authority always do better when they become the boss.

10

CONTROL OVER SELF

Leading With Discipline

Scott Peck wrote, "Discipline is the art of scheduling the pain and pleasure in life in such a way as to confront pain first so as to enhance pleasure later."[1]

The musician who practices is the one also able to play from the heart with a freedom and spontaneity that the undisciplined can only watch and admire.[2]

Our financial woes are not simply related to low incomes or poor economies. John Gatto, New York's Teacher of the Year from 1989-1991, lamented the impact of materialistic thinking on young people: "We need to be more honest and admit that when spending outstrips income, the problem is lack of discipline or priorities, not that we are unable to afford life's necessities."[3]

Discipline sticks to the plan once we're under way, no matter what problems, obstacles, or feelings we face. Discipline lives by principle rather than by emotion. Discipline does what is right even when we don't want to do it. Discipline keeps going even when we are discouraged, or have lost faith, or are facing seemingly impossible odds. Discipline is the making of character; indiscipline, the unmaking of character. Discipline creates a habit, a way of life, a lifestyle.

The world lies at the feet of the disciplined. Motivation is momentary; discipline lasts a lifetime. Whenever we are motivated about doing something, we need to design a sustainable strategy to accomplish the goal. Step-by-step we will get there. Everyone dreams, but only the disciplined will accomplish their dreams. A dream without discipline is the pathway to frustration, anger, and deep disappointment. Just because a dream has divine origins does not guarantee success. That comes because of discipline.

Start disciplined, stay disciplined, and finish disciplined. Discipline is the way of all of life. Morals, finances, attitudes, emotions, relationships, work, devotions—all call for discipline to work properly.

Four areas that call for the highest of discipline in a world of freedom are the tongue, attitudes, the mind, and morals. People who can master these areas will find themselves equipped to gain mastery in every other area of life. In fact, James says that if we can tame our tongue, we are able to maintain control over the rest of our body! (See James 3:2.)

Discipline—Taming the Tongue

We all stumble in many things. If anyone does not stumble in word, he is a perfect man, able also to bridle the whole body.

James 3:2

Our mouth is powerful. It's like a loaded gun, a stick of dynamite, a canon, a bent bow and arrow, a sword, a trowel, a pen, a pouring river. All of these can be good or bad, builders or destroyers, creators of life or bringers of death. It depends on the user. Knowing how to use this small yet powerful member is all-important for us to succeed in life. Our mouth is our power to succeed or fail.

The book of Proverbs is filled with counsel on using our mouths correctly. Here's my commentary on just a few verses from Proverbs and also a few other books:

The lips of the righteous know what is acceptable, but the mouth of the wicked what is perverse.

Prov. 10:32

Good people are recognized by the fact they say things others enjoy. Untrustworthy people are known by their low speech. They say the unacceptable.

The tongue of the wise uses knowledge rightly, but the mouth of fools pours forth foolishness.

Prov. 15:2

Just because we know something doesn't mean we should say it. Knowledge is not enough. Knowing how and when to use what we know is wisdom.

Everyone enjoys a fitting reply; it is wonderful to say the right thing at the right time!

Prov. 15:23 NLT(96)

Giving a good answer brings joy. It is difficult to value something said rightly at the right time. Right words said at the right time have delivered nations, won wars, brought freedom, and secured peace.

The godly think before speaking; the wicked spout evil words.

Prov. 15:28 NLT(96)

Good people think and feel with their heart and mind before they say anything. Fools say the first thing they think of, which will be stupid. The crazy thing is they fail to read the signal that everyone listening is turned off. They just keep on talking without stopping.

The heart of the wise teaches his mouth, and adds learning to his lips.

Prov. 16:23

A wise person's mouth is framed by his heart. He speaks from his heart. There is dialogue between heart and mouth. The lips of the wise are taught by their own heart. We should speak at the pace of our heart, not the pace of our brain. The heart moves slowly but wisely. The brain moves quickly but not wisely. The brain has knowledge. The heart has wisdom. Most people are moved by emotion, then justify their action afterwards with rational reasons from the brain.

If we are ever to be effective communicators, it is imperative our heart is engaged as we speak. Heart speaks to heart, brain to brain. Connecting with people means after I've been speaking with someone, we both feel good, we got something worthwhile at the end of it. We connected. This happens when there is "heart" in our words.

Excellent speech is not becoming to a fool, much less lying lips to a prince.

Prov. 17:7

A fool may try to be a noble person but his speech betrays him. The attempt is a joke. This is bad enough, but worse than this is a leader telling lies. Leaders must be totally committed to truthfulness. The character of a leader must be strong enough to come to the light on each issue they deal with.

A word fitly spoken is like apples of gold in settings of silver.

Prov. 25:11

Appropriate words and articulate speech are like a work of fine art. Receiving a letter from a person who understands the power of upgraded communications is like receiving a priceless work of art. The content and packaging of our communications send powerful messages of the quality of our character. The wise understand what to say and when to say it. Inappropriate speech creates a negative reputation and closes doors of opportunity.

Like the legs of the lame that hang limp is a proverb in the mouth of fools.

Prov. 26:7

Wise statements in the mouth of a person who is not equal to the statement become ineffective because their life fails to endorse their words. Who it is that says a thing is more important than what is said. If what is said is wise, but is said by a person with a poor reputation, the saying falters and isn't received.

...A time to keep silence, and a time to speak.

Eccl. 3:7

A person's silence locates him as much as his speech. There is a time to say nothing. If we don't know a lot about the subject being talked about, the less we say the better. It's time to learn. We reveal our ignorance when we get into conversations beyond our depth. Knowing when to speak and not to speak calls for wisdom.

Our credibility rests on our words coming to pass. Those we lead trust us in a large measure based on the fact that what we say will actually happen. This is not about prophesying. It is about us committing ourselves to doing something, then ensuring we make it happen. We should never let our ego predict the future. A wise man's eyes are in his head (see Eccl. 2:14). He sees the future with his brain not just his heart. What actually happens and what we wish would happen are most often two different things. Our statements about tomorrow need to be sober, not intoxicated with pride.

> *He who covers his sins will not prosper, but whoever confesses and forsakes them will have mercy.*
>
> Prov. 28:13

Covering sins blocks prosperity in our lives. Confessing our wrongs to God brings them into the light. This disarms and dissolves them. The blood of Jesus Christ cleanses us, clearing away all blockages between us, God, and the inevitable upgrading He brings to our lives.

Confession on its own, however, is not enough. We need to stop doing wrong. This brings the mercy of God. This mercy manifests in a life of prosperity.

> *Counsel in the heart of man is like deep water, but a man of understanding will draw it out.*
>
> Prov. 20:5

Most people seeking advice already know what to do within themselves, but for whatever reason they are not yet conscious of that internal counsel. A person with empathy and understanding asks the right questions and draws out this "knowing." A counsellor who has only advice and guidance doesn't bring the person to their own conclusions. If a person discovers their own counsel, they are far more likely to accept it. The wise counsellor provides that environment of empathy where people discover their own inner voice.

There is one who speaks like the piercings of a sword, but the tongue of the wise promotes health.

Prov. 12:18

Right words heal, but cutting words wound people deeply. We live in a world of bitter people. Even though we may think "sticks and stones may break my bones but words will never hurt me," this is not so. Hurtful words leave deep wounds in the soul. People get bitter because these wounds infect their spirit. Words carry spiritual life. If that life is violent, people are damaged within. Successful people understand the power of the tongue and use it to heal and build, not to wound and destroy.

We've all laid on our bed at some time imagining what we're going to say to a person to get back at them. It's like we're sharpening our tongue on a grinder, sparks flying, looking forward to cutting them up with our sword the next time we meet. This is not smart. If we are wise, we will heal the wounded with our words.

A talebearer reveals secrets, but he who is of a faithful spirit conceals a matter.

Prov. 11:13

People don't trust the gossiper. As soon as they have finished talking to you about someone else, they will talk about you to someone else. Trust is built on the ability we have to cover for others. When I'm told something negative but the person telling me attempts to atone for it by saying, "at least I'm being honest," I'd rather they weren't. Honesty doesn't atone for cruelty. Love covers. It hides the things people are ashamed of, their secrets. The trustworthy person doesn't repeat the dark stuff they know about other people.

A soft answer turns away wrath, but a harsh word stirs up anger.

Prov. 15:1

The successful person knows how to defuse volatile situations. When people yell at us, we reply in a low volume with kind words. If we react with yelling and accusations, we are simply gong to exacerbate the problem. Jesus calls peacemakers the children of God (see Matt. 5:9).

...for the wrath of man does not produce the righteousness of God.

James 1:20

Angry words do not solve a problem. Leaders govern their emotions so they bring solutions instead of simply venting their frustrations. Being angry with a person doesn't solve anything, even though we imagine people will behave better if we get upset with them. Even if they do behave better, they will resent the leader and follow begrudgingly. Great leaders are calm in a storm. Their soft words break the bones of a problem.

The wise in heart will be called prudent, and sweetness of the lips increases learning.

Prov. 16:21

When we are training people, we sweeten tough words. This increases their ability to learn. Sour words decrease learning. We may be giving the right information, but people won't be receiving. If our attitude is sweet, so will our words be.

The words of the wise are as goads, and as nails fastened by the masters of assemblies, which are given from one shepherd.

Eccl. 12:11 KJV

This amazing scripture reveals that there are words, both timely and timeless, that leaders of churches can bring to their people that will secure them in the house of God. These words are also called goads, which are the prodding sticks the shepherds would use to motivate and guide their flocks in the right direction.

The faithful pastor who has sought God throughout his life will find messages coming to him that fulfil these criteria. Great churches are built on great messages that come from another dimension than just the mind of a leader. When they sense that the Chief Shepherd Jesus is speaking to His flock, people are attracted to and remain in that assembly.

Faithful are the wounds of a friend, but the kisses of an enemy are deceitful.

Prov. 27:6

Not all hurtful words are bad. A friend who rebukes us is a friend indeed. A friend is someone who has proven him or herself under pressure to be faithful to the relationship. When they decide they need to address something in our lives, we are wise if we heed what they say. Even though they may wound us, when we heal, we will be better people.

In the multitude of words sin is not lacking, but he who restrains his lips is wise.

Prov. 10:19

The person who talks incessantly will eventually say something terrible. They will say something they shouldn't or embarrass themselves by revealing things they ought not. The wise spare their words.

He who answers a matter before he hears it, it is folly and shame to him.

Prov. 18:13

Smart people hear the entire matter before they make a comment. Don't try to finish people's sentences for them. Don't conclude what someone is saying. Hear them out and then make your judgments. Great leaders do not make premature judgments based upon insufficient information. When we say what we think before hearing out the whole story, we may end up being embarrassed. Successful leaders master the art of listening.

Discipline—Ruling Our Attitude

He who is slow to anger is better than the mighty, and he who rules his spirit than he who takes a city.

Prov. 16:32

This proverb reveals that ruling our spirit is basically equivalent to not losing our temper. The Bible permits anger but only with a strong leash. There are moments when anger is appropriate. However, even then we shouldn't lose it. Unrestrained anger quickly takes control of our whole being. We say and do irrational things that bring disastrous damage to ourselves and others.

The person who rules his attitude is considered equal to "taking a city." In fact, the ability to take a city is bound up in the fact that we have mastery of our spirit. This is one of the most demanding disciplines. It is among the most important though, because it is out of our spirit that every issue in life springs (Prov. 4:23).

Conversely, if we are not able to control our spirits, we ourselves will be that city that is "taken."

> *Whoever has no rule over his own spirit is like a city broken down, without walls.*
>
> Prov. 25:28

When anger and its family of bad attitudes rule us, two things happen: we start breaking down internally, and we lose our defense system against onslaughts that come against our mind, health, emotions, and relationships. The out-of-control person lives a broken-down, defenseless life.

The essential functions of a city are:

Government: History teaches plainly that without leadership, any community loses order and becomes chaotic and destructive. If we fail to govern our own lives, we will find exactly the same—chaos and destruction become our norm.

Industry: Failing to discipline our attitude, we jeopardize our potential to generate wealth. Our world revolves around our relationships. If we have a reputation for being a raging bully, difficult to deal with, and generally bad tempered, this closes doors and blocks opportunities for our prosperity. Our motivation evaporates when we are not positive about work. Diligence is basic to generating wealth.

Also, when we are undisciplined in spending, the inevitable debts will crush us.

Communications: Without effective communications, a city is easily destroyed. When we lose our temper, we also lose our mind. Our internal dialogue breaks down along with the external. When we stop communicating with others or ourselves effectively, our city breaks down.

Learning Centers: A city must be able to educate itself to be mature and progressive. Pride fails to learn, thinking it knows all it needs to. There is nothing wrong with a healthy ego—it just needs to be managed so that it doesn't morph into arrogance. It's imperative to humble ourselves by serving others, taking the lower position, giving credit to others, esteeming others better than ourselves. This elevates us, not our posturing as though we are important. Pride breaks our city down.

Rubbish collections: Every city needs to clear its rubbish, otherwise disease is inevitable. Ruling our spirit means we confess sins when we don't want to or find it embarrassing. We get rid of the rubbish we accumulate. Our natural body disposes of waste on a continual and daily basis. We need to do this with our spiritual life as well. The Bible teaches that as we come daily to God in prayer, we should ask forgiveness for any wrongs we've done and also forgive others for anything they have done to us. This is putting out the rubbish. If we allow rubbish to remain in us, it grows rancid inside us, souring our attitude. Paul says we shouldn't let the sun go down on our wrath, meaning that if we have been angry with someone during the day, we should resolve the issue before we sleep (see Eph. 4:26).

Healing Centers: A city must provide healing for its sick. People without control of their attitude lose the ability to self-heal. Emotional disease leads to physical disease. Angry people become depressed. Bitter people grow problems in their bones. Right attitudes bring healing into our systems. Proverbs 17:22 tells us that *"a merry heart does good like a medicine...."* The point is, though, that when we are sick, being merry is not easy. It is a choice, because joy won't come without a decision. But the Bible has told us that joyful people release healing in themselves. We have antibodies that arise to attack invading sickness when we make the choice to have a merry heart.

According to a Dr Renshaw, an associate in the National Health Service Laughter Clinic in Britain in 1991:

> "Hundreds of medical research papers have shown that fun keeps you fit. Laughter lowers blood pressure and massages the heart, lungs, and other vital organs. Laughter triggers the release of an antibody called immunoglobin-A, which boosts the immune system. And even if you do become ill, a good chuckle speeds the healing process."

He also says:

> "The people who live the longest and stay healthiest are those who are the happiest and most creative. Norman Cousins is claimed to be the pioneer of mirth [gaiety or laughter (added by author)] as medicine. Norman was suffering from an incurable disease and to brighten his days began watching Marx Brothers movies. The pleasure of one film gave him two pain free hours of sleep. He checked himself out of the hospital room into a hotel room where he laughed himself back to health."[4]

Every city has buildings, events, and moments dedicated to celebration. These, along with the hospitals, guarantee the health of the community. The person without rule in his spirit lacks this capacity to bring healing and health to his city.

Discipline—Managing Our Mind

William James, the most prominent American psychologist of the nineteenth century was asked to identify the most important finding of the first half-century of university research into the workings of the mind. His reply, "The greatest discovery of my generation is that a human being can alter his life by altering his attitudes of mind."[5]

James Allen, philosopher of the human spirit wrote, "Good thoughts and actions can never produce bad results; bad thoughts and actions can never produce good results."[6] John Maxwell points out that, "One of the reasons people don't achieve their dreams is that they desire to change their results without changing their thinking."[7]

Our minds are the most sophisticated wonderland of human machinery. They can be employed in the noblest pursuits or in devising the most unimaginable evils. As we think, so we are. We choose what we focus our minds upon. We choose what our minds feed on. We choose the heights or the depths our minds will go to. Our lives follow the trajectory of our thoughts. The shape of our mind is the shape of our lives. When we fail to discipline our thoughts, we default to a negative mind-set. We have to set our own minds on the right course. Our mind, like an unattended garden, grows weeds choking out good plants. We can cultivate our minds by reading great books, hearing great speakers, meditating on beautiful things, speaking and writing things that demand the best thinking. The mush of a thousand television shows and glossy gossip magazines "dumb down" our minds to a level below our potential. If we are watching, listening to, and reading a steady diet of junk, we will not remain unaffected. We are what we eat. We become just like the things we spend time thinking about. Let's decide then to feed on things that elevate us.

We set our mind to work—the work of problem solving, discovery, invention, creation, imagining, dreaming, planning, guiding, discerning, remembering, and deciding.

Again and again, the great minds of history and Scripture call on us to give room for thinking, to study, to meditate in the Word of God, ponder the path of our feet, take time out for thinking, rather than letting all the forces of our world do our thinking for us. Bertrand Russell said, "Most people would sooner die than think; in fact, they do so."[8]

Great leaders possess well-ordered minds. This is the mind that tidies its thoughts into lists, priorities, areas, and focus, and then communicates its thoughts so that the people they talk to get unmistakably clear direction. People don't follow uncertain sounds. Uncertain, indecisive minds produce uncertain sounds. The fully persuaded mind brings certainty to its followers and fear to the competition. The key to success is simply being one inch more clearly organized than the next guy.

Discipline—Living Clean

The mass media may present a new morality as the norm, but people still know what is right and what is wrong. Respect is still given to people who are morally clean, even if it is a grudging respect. In the

2004 elections in both the USA and Australia, the media opinion polls revealed immense disdain for both President Bush and Prime Minister Howard over going to war in Iraq. Their position dominated news coverage and was the constant topic of debates.

Yet, after their respective victories, the voters surveyed indicated they voted for the moral stand of the two candidates. It was not the issues of the war or the economy that were the deciders in their campaigns. Their alliance with Christian values and outspoken support for people of faith drew voters to their side. The press didn't see it coming. People still respect right and wrong and will cast their vote behind those with the courage to stand for the right.

Confusion comes at us from all angles. On the one hand, we are told that being sexually promiscuous is normal and should be acceptable. We should cast off old mores or attitudes that have repressed our true selves and our sexual orientations. Yet, in one movie after another, the adulterer is thrown out of the house, relationships are destroyed, and people are deeply hurt by these freedoms.

People ache for the peace that comes into our world from hearts at peace with themselves. This happens only when we do not have a guilty conscience. When leaders live right, people live right. People follow leaders. They justify or condemn their own actions on the basis of those of their leaders. The happiest people are those being led into right living by leaders who have the same private values.

The late Dr. Ed Cole, an apostle of the Christian Men's Movement, once said, "Statesmanship has been swallowed by political expediency. Stewardship in business has been devoured by greed. Philanthropic guardianship has been pillaged by pride. We have sold our moral convictions for profit, power, privilege, or pleasure."[9]

Leaders without double standards are free from clouded signals. Duplicity decimates the power of leadership. A leader with a doubtful private life lacks punch when it comes to assuming strong leadership positions and decisive direction.

Andy Stanley from Atlanta, commenting on the times we live in, says, "Uncertain times require clear directives from those in leadership."[10]

Our lives are the quality of our leading. Our lives are our message. Our lives are our legacy. Great leaders live lives worth remembering and worth modeling ourselves on. The life of Jesus Christ continues to be the greatest life ever lived, and His death the greatest death, for by His life and death, He has provided a way for millions upon millions to follow, which continues to be the case throughout the world today. He has become the captain of our salvation, the apostle of our faith, the greatest leader of all time.

Endnotes

Introduction

[1] Christian Schwarz, *Natural Church Development*, ChurchSmart Resources, 1996.

Chapter 1: Serving Will Serve You Well

[1] Jim Rohn, *The Treasury of Quotes,* Jim Rohn International, p. 90.

[2] Catherine DeVrye, *Good Service Is Good Business,* Career Press, 2001.

[3] Ibid.

[4] *Bits & Pieces*, June 25, 1992.

[5] Laurie Beth Jones, *Jesus CEO*, Hyperion, May 1995, p.91.

[6] John Woolley, and Gerhard Peters, *The American Presidency Project* [online]. Santa Barbara, CA: University of California (hosted), Gerhard Peters (database). Available at http://www.presidency.ucsb.edu/ws/?pid= 9195.

[7] www.quotedb.com/quotes/3280.

[8] Martin Luther King, Jr, "Facing the Challenge of a New Age," December 1956, Montgomery, AL.

[9] Jack Welch, Speech delivered at the New England Council's 1992 Private Sector New Englander of the Year Award, Boston, MA, 11 November, 1992, p.58.

[10] Leon Gettler, *The Age* (Business Section), 29 June 2001, p.5

[11] www.chesscafe.com/text/kmoch02.txt.

[12] www.pediatricservices.com/inspire/inspire30.html.

[13] www.thefreedictionary.com.

Chapter 2: Son of a Gun

[1] Watchman Nee, *The Release of the Spirit,* Christian Fellowship Publishers, June 2000.

Chapter 3: Soldier Through and Through

[1] Edward Gibbon, *The Decline and Fall of the Roman Empire*, Penguin Classics, 1985, p. 66. (Pages 66–85 offer a comprehensive account of the prosperity the Roman leaders brought to their domain.)

[2] Edwin Louis Cole, *Strong Men In Tough Times*, Creation House, 1993.

[3] William Barclay quoted in Gordon McDonald, *Ordering Your Private World*, Highland Books, 1984, p.70.

Chapter 4: Imperative Success

[1] Cynthia Thomas, *Leadership*, Vol. 15, No. 1.

[2] Janet Lowe, *Jack Welch Speaks: Wisdom from the World's Greatest Business Leader*, John Wiley & Sons, 1998, p.170.

[3] Roy H. Williams, *Magical Worlds of the Wizard of Ads*, Bard Press, December 2001, p.159.

[4] Donald T. Phillips, *Lincoln On Leadership: Executive Strategies for Tough Times*, Warner Books, February 1993.

[5] Ibid.

[6] Andy Stanley, *The Next Generation Leader*, Multnomah Publishers, 2003, p.44.

[7] Jack Canfield, Mark Victor Hansen, and Barry Spilchuk, *A Cup of Chicken Soup for the Soul*, Health Communications, Inc., 1996, pp. 64-65.

[8] Bill Hull, *Jesus Christ, Disciplemaker*, Crossway Books, 1992, p.142.

[9] Roy H. Williams, *The Wizard of Ads*, Bard Press, 1998, pp.206-207.

[10] Peter Petre, "The Man Who Brought GE to Life," *Fortune*, 5 January 1986, p.21.

[11] Philip Baker, *Secrets of Super Achievers*, Webb & Partners. 1997, p.18.

[12] http://thinkexist.com/quotation/don-t_go_around_saying_the_world_owes_you_a/168264.html.

[13] Bob Harrison, *Power Points for Success*, Honor Books, 1997, p.37.

[14] Dr Bob Rotella, *Golf is not a Game of Perfect*, Simon & Schuster, 1995, (Appendix: Rotella's Rules).

[15] www.christianheritageworks.com/missions/history3.html.

[16] http://jmm.aaa.net.au/articles/552.htm.

[17] Andy Stanley, *The Next Generation Leader*, Multnomah Publishers, 2003, pp.44, 50.

[18] Roy H. Williams, *The Wizard of Ads*, Bard Press, 1998, p.197.

[19] Stephen Mansfield, *Never Give In: The Extraordinary Character of Winston Churchill*, Cumberland House Publishing, 2002, p.174.

[20] http/www.rtek2000.com/Good/MCSEdiscussion.html#bill.

[21] Dennis E. Waitley, *The Psychology of Winning*, 1984.

[22] Quoted in Robert Andrews, Mary Biggs, Michael Seidel, et al., *The Columbia World of Quotations*, Columbia University Press, 1996.

Chapter 5: Strong as an Ox

[1] Rick Warren, *The Purpose Driven Church*, Zondervan Publishing House, 1995, p.68-69.

[2] Stephen Mansfield, *Never Give In: The Extraordinary Character of Winston Churchill*, Cumberland House Publishing, 2002, pp.114, 116.

[3] http://thinkexist.com/quotatioin/criticism_is_prejudice_made_plausible/208112.html.

[4] http://www.graceonlinelibrary.org/articles/full.asp?id=41%7C%7C29

[5] Andrew Robert Fausset, *Fausset's Bible Dictionary*, Electronic Database, Copyright ©1998 by Biblesoft, All rights reserved.

[6] Roy H. Williams, *Magical Worlds of the Wizard of Ads*, Bard Press, 2001, p.169.

[7] Jim Collins, *Good to Great*, HarperCollins, 2001, p.89.

Chapter 6: Sound Words, Sound Heart

[1] Donald T. Phillips, *Lincoln on Leadership: Executive Strategies for Tough Times*, Warner Books, 1992, p.52.

[2] Bill McArtney, *What Makes a Man*, Navpress, 1992, p.15.

[3] Noel M. Tichy & Stratford Sherman, *Control Your Own Destiny Or Someone Else Will*, Currency Doubleday, 1993, p.148.

[4] Charles Spurgeon, *Lectures to My Students,* Zondervan, 1979, p.225.

[5] http://quote.robertgenn.com/auth_search.php?authid=1348

[6] Robert T. Kiyosaki, *Rich Dad's Guide to Investing*, Warner Business Books, 2000.

[7] Stephen R. Covey, *The 7 Habits of Highly Effective People*, Simon and Schuster, 1989, p.171.

[8] www.quipsmart.com

Chapter 7: Uncommon Sense

[1] Daniel Goleman, Richard Boytzis & Annie McKee, *The New Leaders*, Time Warner, 2003, p.132.

[2] ibid, p.131-132.

[3] ibid, p.133.

[4] http://www.spurgeon.org/treasury/ps023.htm, verse 5.

[5] Herbert Lockyer (ed), *Nelson's Illustrated Bible Dictionary*, Thomas Nelson Publishers, 1986, p.1103.

[6] *Reader's Digest*, March 1993, p.128.

[7] www.geocities.com/cqcumber_99/oddsandends2a.html.

[8] *Today in the Word*, Moody Bible Institute, April 1990, p.27.

[9] Stanley L. Miller, *From the Primitive Atmosphere to the Prebiotic Soup to the Pre-RNA World*, Washington, D.C.: National Aeronautics and Space Administration, 1996.

[10] Charles Colson & Nancy Pearcey, *How Now Shall We Live?*, Tyndale House Publishers, Wheaton, Illinois, 1999, p.149.

[11] Ibid, p.172.

[12] Ibid, op. cit., p.172.

[13] Ibid, p.174.

[14] Daniel Goleman, Richard Boyatzis & Annie McKee, *The New Leaders*, Time Warner Paperbacks, 2003, pp.26-28.

[15] Francis Schaeffer, *Genesis in Space and Time*, InterVarsity Press, 1972, pp.80-83.

[16] Janet Lowe, *Jack Welch Speaks: Wisdom from the world's greatest business leader*, Wiley Publishers, 1998, p.170.

[17] www.quoteworld.org/quotes/3496.

[18] Philip Baker, *Secrets of Super Achievers*, Webb & Partners, 1997, p.99.

[19] Jack Welch, General Electric Annual Meeting, Charlotte, NC, 23 April 1997, p.48.

[20] Egon Zehnder International, *Focus: Value Management*, January 1997, p.84.

[21] Brian Tracy, *Excerpts From the Treasury of Quotes,* yoursuccessstore.com, 1998.

[22] Robert T. Kiyosaki, *Rich Dad's Guide to Investing*, Warner Business Books, 2000.

[23] Edwin Cole, *Maximized Manhood,* Whitaker House, 1982.

[24] www.phoenixmasonry.org/the_builder_1922_may.htm.

[25] Charles Colson & Nancy Pearcey, *How Now Shall We Live?* Tyndale House Publishers, Wheaton, Illinois, 1999, p.16.

[26] http://www.elca.org/lutheranpartners/comment/past/040304.html

[27] http://charactercincinnati.org/Faith/Qualities/Initiative/johnwesley.htm

Chapter 8: Self-Security

[1] Rick Warren, *The Purpose Driven Life*, Zondervan, 2002, p.27.

[2] http://thesaurus.reference.com/browse/image.

[3] Susan Jeffers, "Building Your Self-Esteem—Your Positive Words Will Make You Strong," *Success*, October 1987.

[4] http://findarticles.com/p/articles/mi_m1365/is_7_31/ai_69290621

Chapter 9: An Excellent Spirit

[1] Ken Blanchard & Norman Vincent Peale, *The Power of Ethical Management*, p.231.

[2] Hugh Mackay, *Reinventing Australia*, HarperCollins, 1993.

[3] Sam Walton, www.walmartstores.com.

[4] Laurie Beth Jones, *Jesus CEO*, Hyperion,, 1995, pp.11-12.

[5] Jack Hanes, *His Last Command, Our First Priority*, Megalife Ministries, 2002, p.80.

[6] www.cs.virginia.edu/~robins/quotes.html.

[7] Lecture 10. "On Conversion as Our Aim." http://www.godrules.net/ library/spurgeon/NEW7spurgeon_c12.htm

[8] Charles Colson & Nancy Pearcey, *How Now Shall We Live?*, Tyndale House Publishers, Wheaton, Illinois, 1999, p.137.

[9] *As You Like It* Act ii, scene 7.

[10] Jack Canfield and Mark Victor Hansen, *Chicken Soup for Unsinkable Soul: 101 Inspirational Stories of Overcoming Life's Challenges*, Health Communications, Inc., 1999, pp.297-298.

[11] www.ecw-redcross.org/pdf/bridges-newsletter.pdf.

[12] Catherine DeVrye, *Good Service Is Good Business*, Career Press, 2001.

[13] Hugh MacKay, *Reinventing Australia*, HarperCollins, 1993.

[14] Jack Welch, General Electric Annual Meeting, Charlotte, NC, 23 April 1997, p.49.

[15] Stephen Mansfield, *Never Give In: The Extraordinary Character of Winston Churchill*, Cumberland House Publishing, 2002, p.125.

[16] Donald T. Phillips, *Lincoln On Leadership: Executive Strategies for Tough Times*, Warner Books, 1992.

Chapter 10: Control Over Self

[1] Scott Peck, *The Road Less Traveled*, Arrow Books, 1990, p.18.

[2] Philip Baker, *Secrets of Super Achievers*, Webb & Partners, 1997, p.151.

[3] ibid. p.120.

[4] *The Daily Telegraph*(Sydney, Australia), Monday 24 February, 1997, p.70.

[5] http://www.quotationspage.com/quote/1971.html.

[6] James Allen, *As a Man Thinketh*, p.7.

[7] John C Maxwell, *Thinking for a Change*, Yates & Yates, 2003, p.8.

[8] http://en.thinkexist.com/quotation/most_people_would_sooner_die_ than_ think-in_fact/199743.html

[9] Edwin Louis Cole, "Strong Men In Tough Times," *Charisma*, July 1993, p28 (Adapted from Edwin Louis Cole, *Strong Men In Tough Times*, Creation House, 1993).

[10] Andy Stanley, *The Next Generation Leader*, Multnomah Publishers, 2003, pp.11-12.

Prayer of Salvation

God loves you—no matter who you are, no matter what your past. God loves you so much that He gave His one and only begotten Son for you. The Bible tells us that "…whoever believes in him shall not perish but have eternal life" (John 3:16 NIV). Jesus laid down His life and rose again so that we could spend eternity with Him in heaven and experience His absolute best on earth. If you would like to receive Jesus into your life, say the following prayer out loud and mean it from your heart:

> *Heavenly Father, I come to You admitting that I am a sinner. Right now, I choose to turn away from sin, and I ask You to cleanse me of all unrighteousness. I believe that Your Son, Jesus, died on the cross to take away my sins. I also believe that He rose again from the dead so that I might be forgiven of my sins and made righteous through faith in Him. I call upon the name of Jesus Christ to be the Savior and Lord of my life. Jesus, I choose to follow You and ask that You fill me with the power of the Holy Spirit. I declare that right now I am a child of God. I am free from sin and full of the righteousness of God. I am saved in Jesus' name. Amen.*

If you prayed this prayer to receive Jesus Christ as your Savior for the first time, please contact us on the Web at **www.harrisonhouse.com** to receive a free book.

Or you may write to us at

Harrison House
P.O. Box 35035
Tulsa, Oklahoma 74153

Pastor Phil Pringle is the Senior Minister of one of Australia's fastest growing, exciting, and powerful churches. In 1980, Phil and his wife, Christine, arrived in Sydney, Australia, from New Zealand armed with faith and a vision to build a contemporary, vibrant church that would grow and impact a city for Christ.

Today, 23 years later, Christian City Church Oxford Falls, is one of Australia's largest churches, with over 4,000 members—quickly heading toward 5,000 members. The church is made up of many departments, each reflecting Pastor Phil's original passion to liberate a city and nation through the life-transforming Gospel of Jesus Christ through every available relevant means. Pastor Phil has always projected the vision of planting new congregations, especially in major cities around the world.

Today, Dr. Pringle oversees the approximately 1,200 churches that make up Christian City Church International throughout the world, a significant proportion of which have been planted directly from Christian City Church Oxford Falls.

Christian City Church Oxford Falls has a School of Ministry, developing powerful ministries for the future; a School of Creative Arts, developing ministries in the Arts; Pastoral Care and Counselling College; the International School of the Church, which trains pastors and teams to plant churches and take the churches to new levels of growth; a business course; Jesus Television, a television studio creating high quality material for weekly broadcasts; Seam of Gold, a record label, producing and distributing worldwide original and contemporary praise and worship coming out of this congregation.

The keys to this growth are vision, faith, moving in the Spirit, and development of leadership. Phil is a pastor, preacher, songwriter, artist, author, and leader. He maintains an uncompromised passion to see cities changed by a contemporary, relevant, and anointed church of God; and he shares his message in a down-to-earth manner, using humor and a sensitivity to the dynamics of the Holy Spirit.

In his meetings, Phil has seen powerful moves of God break out, the glory of God filling the atmosphere, and people touched by the Holy Spirit. As a result, many have been saved and lives have been totally changed.

To contact Phil Pringle
please write to:

Pax Ministries
Locked Bag 8
Dee Why NSW 2099
AUSTRALIA
Email: pax@ccc.org.au

*Please include your prayer requests
and comments when you write.*

Other Books by Dr. Pringle

Faith

Healing the Wounded Spirit

Dead For Nothing?

Keys to Financial Excellence The Leadership Files Vol. 1

The Leadership Files Vol. 2

You the Leader

Books by Chris Pringle

Jesse—Found In Heaven